Better Homes and Gardens®

HOME
CANNING
COOK BOOK

Express your appreciation of special friends by presenting them with a jar of homemade jam or jelly. Plan ahead at jelly-making time and pack these flavorful products in heatproof glasses suitable for gift giving.

BETTER HOMES AND GARDENS BOOKS

Editorial Director: Don Dooley
Managing Editor: Malcolm E. Robinson   Art Director: John Berg
Asst. Managing Editor: Lawrence D. Clayton   Asst. Art Director: Randall Yontz
Food Editor: Nancy Morton
Senior Food Editor: Joyce Trollope
Associate Editors: Rosemary C. Hutchinson, Sharyl Heiken, Elizabeth Strait
Assistant Editors: Sandra Granseth, Diane Jesse, Catherine Penney
Designers: Harijs Priekulis, Faith Berven

CONTENTS

Our seal assures you that every recipe in *Home Canning Cook Book* is endorsed by the Better Homes and Gardens Test Kitchen. Each recipe is tested for family appeal, practicality, and deliciousness.

BY WAY OF INTRODUCTION

Preserving food has been a problem for man from the earliest times. If he lived in the arctic, he could freeze it. If he lived in the desert, he could dry it. And if he lived near the ocean, he could pickle it in salt water. Otherwise, he ate as much food as he could before it spoiled.

The big breakthrough in food preservation came in 1810 when a French confectioner named Appert developed a method of preserving food in a bottle. He had no idea why heating food in a sealed container preserved it. That knowledge came years later. Nevertheless, his work had a profound effect on the development of food storage.

Although the canning process eventually went commercial, canning food at home retains its importance. What was both a necessity and a source of satisfaction to the farm wife and avid gardener now extends beyond the rural scene. Urban homemakers are experiencing the same sense of accomplishment from home canning.

The freezing story, although less dramatic, is equally important. Freezing foods was commonplace for centuries in cold climates, but not until the advent of electricity, home freezers, and superior wrapping materials did it become practical in home kitchens everywhere.

In this book the editors have detailed in up-to-the-minute, simple-to-follow instructions how to can and freeze almost everything and how to make jellies and pickles. You'll also come across helpful tip boxes, and as a plus, recipes that have been specially developed to utilize home-canned ingredients. So, for any homemaker who wants to enjoy her favorite fruits, vegetables, and meats year-round, *Home Canning Cook Book* is a must.

Can ahead for tomorrow's good eating

← *Display your home-canned foods with pride. An impressive array of tasty jams, relishes, fruits, or vegetables awaits your serving pleasure. Not only is the canning a satisfying do-it-yourself project, but the foods canned bring variety to mealtime throughout the year.*

Capture nature's goodness from the garden by canning luscious fruits and vegetables. Enjoy them long after the growing season is over. Whether you harvest your own or purchase the abundant produce, canning these foods is a do-it-yourself project to be proud of.

Begin your adventures with home canning in the spring when tender asparagus and pink rhubarb first come on the scene. Then, add to your storehouse throughout the summer and fall as each fruit or vegetable is at its peak of flavor.

Canning Techniques

Never done any home canning before? Don't let that stand in your way. Just follow the Canning Basics on the next few pages. All aspects of canning are explained, and there are plenty of how-to photographs to show you just what to do.

For ease of reference, the foods to be canned are grouped according to whether they are high or low in natural acidity. Fruits and High-Acid Vegetables are first. Next come the Low-Acid Vegetables. Then the Meats, Fish, and Poultry.

Finally, look to the Editors' Choice recipes at the end of the chapter for ways to serve your home-canned foods.

Golden Pineapple Spears *(page 24), bright* Green → Beans *(page 30), and ruby-red* Beets *(page 30) are ready for convenient storage on the kitchen shelf now and for mealtime enjoyment in days to come.*

CANNING BASICS

Join the ranks of homemakers who have discovered that canning is one of the easiest and most satisfying ways to ensure having your favorite fruits, vegetables, and meats year-round. While turning out a marvelous array of jars packed with fruits and vegetables is a natural activity for the home gardener, the smart shopper can do the same. And it isn't difficult. All you need is the basic equipment and an understanding of why canning works.

What Canning Does

All fresh fruits, vegetables, and meats are perishable. With the exception of some fruits and a few vegetables, fresh foods must be prepared and served soon after harvesting or they begin to spoil, to change color and flavor, and ultimately to decompose. This is nature's plan. A few day's storage in the refrigerator will delay these processes, but it takes something drastic to halt them completely. Canning does this by heating food in sealed containers. The heat destroys the troublesome organisms and the sealed containers prevent recontamination of the processed food.

Use standard jars for canning

For home-canned products use only standard mason jars and the lids designed to fit them. Stock jars—those in which you buy mayonnaise, peanut butter, or commercially canned foods—are not satisfactory for home canning.

The glass in stock jars has not been tempered to stand up under the combination of time and temperature used in home canning. The jars may break midway through processing. Also, since the mouth opening and threading on the neck of the jars do not match either zinc-lined caps or the metal lids and screw bands, the jars will not seal.

By following the basic canning rules, you prevent molds, yeasts, and bacteria that are normally present in the soil, air, and on work surfaces in the kitchen from causing spoilage or illness. You also destroy the enzymes that cause undesirable color, texture, and flavor changes in uncooked produce and meats. While these changes are not harmful, they do make the foods less appetizing.

For canning to be effective, you must have the proper combination of temperature and time. While 212° in the boiling water bath is sufficient to destroy the harmful organisms in a high-acid food, you must process low-acid foods at 240° to achieve the same result. In order to do this you'll need two basic pieces of equipment: a water-bath canner for processing high-acid foods and a pressure canner for low-acid foods. Then, process each food for the required number of minutes.

Canners

The water-bath canner. This, the least expensive type of canner, actually is just a large, deep kettle fitted with a rack and a lid. Buy one specially made for canning, or use a big kettle you already have. Make sure that it is deep enough to allow one or two inches of water to bubble vigorously over the top of the jars during processing. The cover on the canner prevents the steam from billowing out into the kitchen. Use the water-bath canner when processing fruits, fruit juices, high-acid vegetables such as tomatoes, and sauerkraut, pickles, or relishes.

The pressure canner. This is a more sophisticated piece of equipment, similar to a pressure cooker. It consists of a heavy, seamless kettle with a rack and a locking lid with gasket, pressure gauge, and safety valve. The gauge may be either a spring dial or a weight. When you maintain 10 pounds pressure in the canner for the specified time, the food is being processed at a temperature of 240°. The pressure canner is essential for canning foods that are low in natural acidity. This includes most vegetables, and all meats or fish.

If you have a pressure cooker with a rack as part of your cooking utensils, you can substitute it for a pressure canner for processing pint jars. However, the cooker must have a gauge that will maintain 10 pounds pressure. Add 20 minutes to the processing time listed in charts and recipes.

Containers and Lids

Just as there are two basic styles of canners, so, too, are there two basic types of containers: glass jars and metal cans. Each has specially designed lids that ensure a complete seal.

Glass canning jars, also known as mason jars after their nineteenth-century American inventor, John L. Mason, are the standard jars to use in home canning. (See tip box.) These reusable jars are produced in a variety of sizes, suitable for both home canning and home freezing. (See photo, page 10.)

The glass in these jars is tempered in order to withstand either the heat and pressure of a pressure canner, or the below-zero cold of a freezer. In addition, the jars have a threaded mouth so that either the zinc cap and rubber ring or the flat metal lid with screw band makes an airtight closure.

The zinc cap with porcelain lining and rubber ring was the first screw cap developed for Mr. Mason's jars. (Although zinc caps and rubber rings are still produced, their popularity is declining.) To use them, wet and slip the flexible rubber ring over the mouth of the jar and fit it snugly against the shoulder of the jar. Next, screw the zinc cap down firmly against the rubber, then unscrew it about ¼ inch. This allows for expansion of the metal in the cap during processing. Immediately after the hot jars come out of the canner, grasp the jar and cap firmly with potholders and tighten the caps to complete the seal.

Three canners. On the left is a pressure canner containing jars of cut green beans. It has a spring dial-gauge on its cover for registering pressure. On the right is a pressure canner that makes use of a weight gauge. In the rear is a boiling water-bath canner containing peaches.

Canning jars and jelly glasses. Back row: Wide-mouth quart, 1½ pint, and regular quart jars. Middle row: Specialty half-pint, wide-mouth pint, regular pint, and regular half-pint. Front row: Flat jelly glass with lid; wide-mouth metal lid with screw band, specialty jelly glass with lid, regular metal lid with screw band, and zinc cap with rubber ring.

The flat metal lid with sealing compound and metal screw band is the most popular type of cap for home-canned products. To use, place the center lid on the rim of the jar with the sealing compound next to the glass. Screw the band firmly to hold the lid in place. Do not loosen. During processing, air is exhausted from the jars so that as the jar cools, a vacuum pulls the lid tightly against the rim of the jar. When the jar is completely cooled and sealed, remove the screw band. The vacuum and the sealing compound will maintain the seal.

The screw bands may be reused as long as they are not bent out of shape, but the flat lids are designed for one-time usage. Since each brand of lid has a different sealing compound, follow package directions exactly when preparing the lids for canning.

Metal cans are also used for home canning in some parts of the country. However, since distribution is not extensive, tin containers and lids for home canning are becoming difficult to locate. The purchase of special closing equipment to seal the cans is also necessary. An additional problem arises over processing times. Can and jar sizes are not the same and rate of heat penetration is different for tin and glass. Thus, processing times in recipes and charts for jars are not usable for cans. If you are using cans, follow directions that accompany the equipment you have, or contact the Extension Service in your county for processing times for tin cans.

Regardless of the type of canner or container to be used, the foods are prepared and packed in the same way.

Getting Food Ready to Can

Fruits and vegetables: Preserving the goodness of fruits and vegetables begins with the product itself. The higher its quality and the shorter the time period between garden and canner, the better the final canned goods.

Choose only fresh, ripe-yet-firm fruits and young, tender vegetables for canning. Sort them according to size, color, and maturity, as this ensures even cooking during processing.

Wash all fruits and vegetables thoroughly, but gently. Do small lots under running water or through several changes of water. If you use the latter method, remember to lift the produce out of the water with each change so that dirt doesn't resettle on the food. This procedure is particularly important because garden soil contains the illness-causing bacteria that are most difficult to destroy.

When washing is completed, work quickly to do the necessary peeling, coring, or cutting so that the food can go into the jars without long periods of soaking or standing. It is while standing that water-soluble vitamins wash out and the food soaks up water.

Meats, poultry, and fish: Handle all these products carefully to avoid contamination. Chill freshly slaughtered meats and poultry immediately to 40° or lower. Refrigerate purchased products. Chill dressed fish and soak it about 1 hour in a salt solution.

Filling the Jars

Certain canning procedures are the same whether processing is done in a water-bath canner or a pressure canner. First, examine jars for nicks around the rim. (See photo A.) Today's mason jars do not need to be boiled or sterilized. Just give them a sudsy wash and thorough rinse. Then, pour boiling water over the jars and allow them to stand in hot water till time to fill.

For most foods either the raw-pack or the hot-pack method may be used. In the recipes and charts throughout this book, both methods are given unless a particular food is best done only one way. In that case, the most satisfactory method is specified.

Raw Pack: Pack the uncooked food into containers. Then, add a boiling liquid such as syrup, water, or fruit juice to desired depth.

Hot Pack: Partially cook the food before packing it into containers. Then, add boiling liquid to fill the jars.

The following steps apply to both raw pack and hot pack.

1. Pack foods into hot jars, leaving the headspace—room at the top—specified for the particular product: ½-inch headspace for fruits and non-starchy vegetables; and 1-inch headspace for starchy vegetables and meats. Put a cloth under the jar to prevent it from slipping and to catch any spills. (See photo B.)

Inspect each canning jar by running your finger around the rim. Edges must be smooth to ensure a good seal. Discard jars that are nicked or cracked.

Spoon cleaned and cut beans into jar with slotted spoon. When filled, shake jar gently to settle the contents. Be sure to leave specified headspace.

Carefully pour the boiling water, cooking liquid, or syrup over the food, leaving desired amount of headspace. Grasp hot jar firmly with a potholder.

Gently work the blade of a table knife or flexible spatula around inside the filled jar to eliminate air bubbles. Add more boiling liquid if needed.

With a damp cloth or piece of paper towel wipe off the rim of the jar to remove all food particles or traces of syrup from this important sealing edge.

2. Ladle boiling water, cooking liquid, or syrup over the food; leave specified headspace. The jar will get hot, so use a potholder to protect your fingers. (See photo C.)

3. Use a flexible spatula or table knife to work out any air bubbles in the filled jar. Move the blade around gently so as not to break up the pieces of food. (See photo D.) Add more boiling liquid if necessary.

4. Wipe off the rim of the jar with an absorbent cloth or paper towel. (See photo E.) Bits of food or syrup on the rim could prevent a perfect seal after processing.

5. Prepare the lids according to the manufacturer's directions. When using the flat metal lid, place it compound side down, squarely on the rim of the jar. Add the metal band and screw down until it is firm and tight. (See photo F.)

6. Using a jar lifter or long-handled tongs, transfer the filled jar to the canner. Complete filling, covering, and placing each jar in the canner before filling another. (See photo G.) Jars will start to heat as they wait.

Processing Methods

Of the three best-known canning methods—water-bath, pressure, and open-kettle—the first two are recommended and the third has limited usage. Water-bath and pressure canning are the safest to use for particular foods while open-kettle canning is reserved for jams and jellies. A fourth method, oven canning, is dangerous and should never be used.

Water-bath canning is recommended for most fruits; the high-acid vegetables such as tomatoes and ripe pimiento peppers; sauerkraut; and all pickles and relishes. Use either a raw pack or a hot pack when filling jars.

1. Set the water-bath canner containing a rack on your kitchen range. Fill the kettle with four to five inches of water. Place cover on canner and start heating the water over high heat. Also, start heating additional water, which eventually will be used to fill the canner after all of the jars are in place, in a teakettle or other large container. Since this initial heating may take some time, it is a good idea to get it started early.

2. Prepare the sugar syrup if it is to be used. (See page 22 for correct proportions of sugar and water.) Having the syrup ready will ex-

Follow package directions for preparing the metal sealing lids. Place the lid so that the sealing compound rests on the rim. Screw on metal bands.

G

Have water heating in the canner on the range. As each jar is filled and closed, place on the canner rack, using a jar lifter or long-handled tongs.

H

Add hot water to bring the level in the canner one or two inches over the tops of the jars. Cover the canner and heat the water to a brisk rolling boil.

Altitude correction— water-bath canning

Add 1 minute to processing for each 1,000 feet above sea level when the time specified is 20 minutes or less. Add 2 minutes to processing for each 1,000 feet above sea level if the time called for is more than 20 minutes. **Do not raw pack vegetables for processing at altitudes above 6,000 feet.**

---

pedite getting the fruit into the jars for processing. When the syrup is prepared, keep it warm but not boiling until you're ready to pour it over the fruit. Boiling the syrup for any length of time will evaporate some of the water and make it more concentrated.

3. Prepare the fruits or vegetables to be canned, following the directions given in the appropriate chart or recipe. Information about fruits and high-acid vegetables begins on page 18. Recipes for pickles and relishes begin on page 58. You can also check the index for the page number of a specific food.

4. Refer to the step-by-step directions and photographs on pages 11 and 12 when you are ready to fill the jars.

5. When the water in the canner is hot, fill each jar and place it on the rack in the canner. The contents of each jar will begin to warm up while you are filling the next jar. Make sure jars do not touch. Replace the cover on the canner each time you add a jar so that a minimum of steam escapes.

6. When last jar has been added to canner, check water level in the canner. Using the boiling water that was heated in teakettle, fill canner so water is one to two inches over tops of jars. (See photo H.) Place cover on canner and continue heating till water comes to brisk rolling boil. **(See page 73 for exceptions when processing pickles or relishes.)**

7. Now, start counting the processing time. Times for various-sized jars are given in each chart or recipe. Remember that the times listed are for foods canned at sea level. The altitude will affect the timing needed. Make adjustments as described in the tip box.

When processing time is up, transfer hot jars to a rack to cool. Area should be draft-free with ample space to allow air to circulate around jars.

8. Adjust the heat under the canner so the water will boil gently during the entire processing time. Have a teakettle of boiling water nearby in case the water level in the canner drops. If the water stops boiling when you add water, stop counting the processing time, turn up the heat, and wait for a full boil before resuming the counting.

9. When processing time is up, turn heat off under canner. Use a jar lifter or long-handled tongs to transfer hot jars to rack in draft-free cooling area. Leave space between jars for air circulation. (See photo I.)

Pressure canning is absolutely necessary for processing foods that are naturally low in acid. These foods include corn, beans of all kinds, carrots, beets, greens, and most garden vegetables plus all meats, poultry, and fish. It takes more than boiling water temperatures to destroy botulism-causing organisms when they are present in low-acid foods.

At 10 pounds pressure in the canner, the temperature reaches 240°. The processing time specified for each food ensures adequate heat penetration. As an extra safeguard, boil these foods at least 10 minutes before tasting or serving (corn or spinach 20 minutes). Never serve these products cold from the jar.

1. Well before canning day, read the instruction booklet packed with the canner. If canner has a spring-dial gauge, have it checked for accuracy. The Extension Service in your county can tell you the nearest testing location. If gauge is 5 pounds off, replace it. If less than 5 pounds off, adjust pressure.

2. Assemble canner and basket. Set the canner on your kitchen range. Add 2 or 3 inches of boiling water or the amount recommended by the manufacturer. Turn heat on low.

3. Prepare vegetables or meats to be canned by following the directions given in the appropriate chart or recipe. Information about low-acid vegetables begins on page 28. Directions for canning various types of meat, fish, and poultry begin on page 38.

4. Refer to directions and photos on pages 11 and 12 when you are ready to fill the jars.

5. As each jar is filled, place it in the canner. Be sure the jars do not touch. The contents of the jar will begin to warm up while you are preparing the next jar. Always do like products and jar sizes in one canner load. Although it is more efficient to fill the canner to capacity for each processing, a smaller number of jars does not affect processing time or quality.

6. Cover the canner and lock securely. Turn the heat up to high. Watch the open vent or pet cock to see when the steam starts to come from the pipe. Reduce the heat so that the steam flows freely at a moderate rate. Let the steam flow steadily for 10 minutes. It will take this long to exhaust the air from inside the canner and the jars.

7. Close the vent and bring up the pressure. Depending on the age and model of the canner, this may involve several steps. Refer to your owner's manual for specific instructions.

**Altitude correction—
pressure canner**

Pounds of pressure given in charts and recipes apply up to 2,000 feet above sea level. Make the following adjustments for the type of gauge on canner.

Spring-dial gauge: For each additional 2,000 feet add 1 pound of pressure.

Weight gauge: Above 2,000 feet use 15 pounds pressure instead of 10. **Do not raw pack vegetables for processing at altitudes above 6,000 feet.**

8. Turn the heat up to high again. Maintain this heat until the 10 pounds pressure has been reached. Then, adjust heat to maintain a constant pressure. This constant 10 pounds pressure throughout processing is important because any fluctuation will draw the liquid out of the jars. Also, if the pressure drops, you will have to stop counting processing time until the desired pressure is regained.

9. Count processing time from the moment 10 pounds pressure is reached. Times for quarts, pints, or half-pints are given in charts or recipes. These times are calculated for canning at sea level, so make altitude adjustments, if needed. (See the tip box.)

10. Turn off the heat at the end of processing time. If you are using an electric range, move the canner off the unit. Set the canner out of drafts on a wire rack or wooden board. Allow pressure to return to normal of its own accord. This will take 20 to 25 minutes. Do not run water over the canner or rush cooling.

11. You can tell that the pressure is down when the dial gauge registers zero and the safety plug is normal (see photo A), or when no steam is visible when the weight gauge is nudged gently. (See photo B.) When the pressure is down, remove the regulators or open the pet cock and unlatch the cover of the canner. Be sure to lift the cover so that it opens away from you. (See photo C.)

12. Observe the jars in the canner. If the food is still boiling vigorously, wait a few minutes before removing the jars. Place jars 2 to 3 inches apart on a rack, folded towel, or wooden board in a draft-free area.

Pressure cookers, also known as pressure saucepans, may be used for canning pint jars *if* the pan has a rack and an accurate gauge that will maintain 10 pounds pressure. Read instructions that came with the pressure cooker.

1. Follow steps 1 through 6 under pressure canning, *except* cut to 1 minute the time needed to exhaust the air.

2. Close the vent and bring up pressure to 10 pounds. Add 20 minutes to the processing time given in charts for pints in a pressure canner. This time makes up for the faster heating and cooling periods in the cooker.

3. After processing, let the pressure return to zero before opening cooker. Do not put cooker under cold running water.

4. Unlatch and remove cover. Transfer jars.

On canners with the spring-dial gauge, wait until the indicator has returned to zero (about 20 to 25 minutes) before removing the pressure regulator.

On canners with a weight gauge, let the canner cool 20 to 25 minutes before nudging the gauge gently. If no steam is visible, lift off gauge.

Unlatch canner carefully. Open it away from you to avoid a blast of hot steam. If food in jars is bubbling, wait briefly before removing the jars.

Open-kettle canning is used today only for making jellies and jams. (See page 58.) Formerly, it was common practice to can peaches, tomatoes, and pickles by putting boiling food and syrup or brine in sterilized jars and sealing them. Unfortunately, the spoilage rate was high. Neither the sugar in the fruit syrup nor the acid in the tomatoes or brine was concentrated enough to prevent spoilage of these products. Now, extra heat processing in a water bath is recommended for these products.

Oven processing should not be used. The food in the center of the jars does not get hot enough to be safe to eat and the variable heat in an oven could cause the jars to explode. Processing in a microwave oven holds promise for the future, but to date, safe processing times have not been established.

Testing the Seal

Regardless of the processing method, the job is not done until you know the jar has sealed. You may hear some loud snaps while the jars are cooling. The sound occurs when the vacuum in the jar suddenly pulls down the metal lid to make an airtight seal. However, sealing is not always accompanied by a loud noise. It can take place as you press the center of the lid on a cooled jar. If the dip in the lid holds, the jar is sealed.

Test for the seal by looking for the dip in the lid and feeling it with your fingers. (See photo below.) Or, tap the lid lightly with a metal spoon. A sealed jar with no food touching the lid has a clear ringing sound.

Any jar that has not sealed must be repacked and reprocessed with a new lid for the full length of time. If just one jar didn't seal, refrigerate the food and serve it within a day or two. If the jar has sealed, but the liquid level is low, do not open the jar to add liquid. This breaks the seal.

Once you are satisfied that the jar has sealed, remove the metal screw band. It has served its purpose. In fact, tightening the band at this point could loosen the sealing compound and let air into the jar.

Labeling

Even though home-canned foods are visible through the glass, it is amazing how easy it is to forget details about the seasonings used and the date canned. So, to avoid aggravation later on, write pertinent facts on the lid of each jar with a felt-tip pen, or affix gummed labels.

Storing

Canned foods that have been processed correctly and stored properly will keep for a considerable length of time. A dark, dry place with temperatures below 70° is the ideal location. Home-canned products will lose quality rapidly if stored in a warm room.

Detecting Spoilage

Inspect each jar carefully before serving home-canned foods. If food was underprocessed, yeast and bacteria may not be destroyed. Some microorganisms can grow in an airtight jar. Detecting their presence is a matter of using your eyes, nose, and good sense.

Leakage from jars, patches of mold, and a foamy or murky appearance are visible signs that the product should be discarded. The odor from the opened jar should be pleasant and characteristic of the product canned. If it doesn't look or smell right, do not use it.

A curving down in the lid identifies a sealed jar. The seal can also be tested by tapping the lid with a metal spoon and listening for the ringing sound.

Good sense is important when preparing home-canned vegetables and meats. If the foods were incorrectly processed, it is possible that botulism-causing bacteria, if present, were not destroyed. These bacteria can grow in a closed jar. As they multiply, they produce a deadly toxin. The toxin does not necessarily change the appearance or smell of the food, although an off-odor may show up when the product is boiled. If you have any doubts, destroy the food. Fortunately, the toxin is destroyed by boiling the food, uncovered, for at least 10 minutes (20 minutes for corn and spinach). To be on the safe side, you should never taste low-acid foods cold from the jar. If the product looks and smells good after the suggested boiling, it is safe to eat.

Canning Problems

Canning difficulties tend to fall into several broad categories. They include a poor seal, spoilage, color change, foods that float, sediment in the jars, and a loss of liquid. Some can be prevented by following the step-by-step procedures presented earlier in this chapter. Others, which merely make the food less attractive, are related to the ripeness of fruit and vegetables, the physical change in the food during processing, or the chemical reaction between the food and canning liquid. Read the following to find out what causes a particular problem.

Jars do not seal because:

The jar was filled too full; consequently, the lid did not close properly.

The jar rim was chipped or the rim was not adequately wiped off after filling. Particles of food came between the sealing compound and the rim of the jar.

Jar lids were not used according to the manufacturer's directions. The lids were either too hot or too cold for a good seal.

A scratch across the sealing compound left an air space that prevented complete sealing.

Screw band was bent or rusty and did not hold lid firmly against rim of jar.

Screw band was tightened after the jar was removed from the canner.

Foods spoil because:

Pressure in canner was not maintained at 10 pounds during processing. This happened because the pressure gauge was not accurate, the heat under the canner was too low and allowed the pressure to drop below the necessary 10 pounds, or no altitude correction was made at elevations above 2,000 feet.

Air was not sufficiently exhausted from pressure canner before the regulator was placed over the vent to build up necessary pressure.

Water in water-bath canner was not kept at a full boil throughout entire processing time, or the water level in the canner dropped below the tops of the jars.

Foods change color because:

Foods were too long in preparation.

Food was not processed long enough to destroy the enzymes that affect color.

Foods were overprocessed.

Liquid in the jars did not completely cover food. Exposed portions became discolored.

Air bubbles were not removed.

Fruits such as apples and pears were not treated with ascorbic acid color keeper.

High color in foods such as beets or cherries dissolved in the liquid or syrup.

Chemical changes took place in the coloring matter of the fruit or vegetable.

Food was stored in too warm a place or where the light was exceptionally strong.

Foods float because:

Food was packed too loosely in the jar.

Syrup was too heavy for the fruit.

Raw-pack products tend to float more than those that have some precooking. More air remains in the tissues of uncooked food at the time it goes into the jar.

Food was processed too long.

Fruit was too ripe.

Sediment collects in bottom of jars because:

Minerals present in the water used for precooking foods or for filling the jar settled out.

Table salt with an anti-caking ingredient was used in place of pickling salt.

Starch in corn and beans settled out.

Fruits were overripe.

Liquid is lost or is low because:

Food was packed too tightly or jars were too full. The product boiled over and started a siphoning action.

Air bubbles were not removed.

Water was less than one inch over the tops of the jars in a water-bath canner.

Pressure in pressure canner fluctuated during processing time.

Starchy foods absorbed water.

FRUITS AND
HIGH-ACID VEGETABLES

Besides the convenience and eating enjoyment of having home-canned foods on hand, there is a sense of personal satisfaction every time you open and serve a jar of fruit, fruit juice or syrup, or tomato products. (Remember that for canning purposes tomatoes are grouped with the high-acid fruits.)

Getting Fruits Ready

Plan to can only firm, ripe fruits at their peak of quality. Work quickly and handle them gently because the right stage of maturity is also when fruits are the most fragile.

Thorough washing is important, but do not let cleaned fruit stand long in water or some of the food value will be lost. Work with small batches of fruit, just enough for one jar or one canner load at a time.

Fresh peaches and apricots peel easier if they are dipped in boiling water for a minute.

Some peeled and cut-up fruits have a tendency to darken. However, using a color keeper will solve this problem. (See tip box.)

Amount of Sweetness

One distinct advantage of home-canned fruits is that they can be as sweet or unsweet as family preference dictates. The directions given in each chart or recipe for syrup-packed fruits specify one or more sweetness levels. You may substitute any of the four syrups listed at the top of the chart on page 20. Ranked from not-so-sweet to sweet, they are very light, light, medium, and heavy. Or, you may omit the sugar. (See tip box, page 23.)

A trio of elegant desserts

← *Bring out the crystal and silver for* Minted Pears *(page 24),* Rosy Fruit Cocktail *(page 24), or a pretty pie made with* Apple Pie Filling *(page 25). You'll be proud to serve these handsome desserts.*

Adding color keeper to fruits

Fruits such as apples, apricots, peaches, and pears will darken while being prepared for canning. Prevent this by dropping the peeled, cut-up fruit in water containing an ascorbic acid color keeper. Follow directions on package for proportions of color keeper to water.

You also can use a solution of 2 tablespoons salt and 2 tablespoons vinegar or lemon juice per gallon of water. However, as the vinegar mixture may affect the flavor of the fruit, rinse the fruit thoroughly before packing it into jars.

Packing the Jars

After the fruit has been cleaned, peeled, cored, or otherwise prepared according to the recipe instructions, you are ready to fill the jars. Where there is a choice, you'll need to decide whether to use a raw pack or hot pack for the fruit. Complete how-to information and photographs for both methods begin on page 11. Berries are one of the few exceptions to step #6. Because berries are so very fragile, put all of the jars into the canner at once instead of one by one when filled.

Water-Bath Processing

One of the reasons home-canned peaches and tomatoes are so popular is that the water-bath canner is easy to use. It works equally well for the other fruits, fruit juices, syrups, and butters in this chapter, too. Whether you are a first-time canner or a seasoned veteran, you'll find helpful information and step-by-step photographs for using a water-bath canner beginning on page 12. Follow the timetables carefully and success will be yours.

Canning Fruits

Fruit	Preparation of Fruit	Water bath in minutes (pints)	Water bath in minutes (quarts)
	Very Light Syrup: 1 cup sugar to 4 cups water = 4¾ cups *Light Syrup:* 2 cups sugar to 4 cups water = 5 cups *Medium Syrup:* 3 cups sugar to 4 cups water = 5½ cups *Heavy Syrup:* 4¾ cups sugar to 4 cups water = 6½ cups Boil sugar and water together 5 minutes. Skim if needed.		
Apples *(Allow 2½ to 3 pounds for each quart)* *(Allow 6 to 7 pounds to make 6 pints)*	*Hot Pack:* Prepare syrup; keep hot but not boiling. Wash, peel, core, and cut apples in pieces. While preparing, add color keeper (see tip, page 19). Bring syrup to boiling. Boil apples in syrup 5 minutes. Pack hot apples in hot jars, leaving ½-inch headspace. Cover with boiling syrup, leaving ½-inch headspace. Adjust lids. Process.	15	20
	Applesauce: Wash, quarter, and core apples; add color keeper (see tip, page 19). Combine apples and 4 cups water, cover, bring to boiling. Simmer till very tender, 15 minutes. Press apples through food mill. Return applesauce to kettle and add 2 to 2½ cups sugar. Cook and stir over low heat till sugar dissolves. Bring to boiling; stir to prevent sticking. Taste for sweetness. Pack hot into jars, leaving ½-inch headspace. Adjust lids. Process.	10	10
Apricots *(Allow 1½ pounds as purchased for each quart)*	*Raw Pack:* Prepare the syrup; keep hot but not boiling. While preparing apricots, add color keeper (see tip, page 19). Wash fruit; halve and pit enough to fill one jar at a time. Peeling is optional. Pack into hot jars, leaving ½-inch headspace. Bring syrup to boiling. Cover fruit with syrup, leaving ½-inch headspace. Adjust lids. Process.	25	30
	Hot Pack: Prepare as above, but heat fruit through in syrup. Pack hot apricots into hot jars, leaving ½-inch headspace. Cover with boiling syrup, leaving ½-inch headspace. Adjust lids. Process in boiling water bath.	20	25
Berries, except strawberries *(Allow 1½ to 3 pounds for each quart)*	*Raw Pack:* Use for raspberries and other soft berries. Prepare syrup; keep hot but not boiling. Wash fruit; drain. Fill hot jars, leaving ½-inch headspace. Bring syrup to boiling. Cover berries with boiling syrup; leave ½-inch headspace. Adjust lids. Process in boiling water bath.	10	15
	Hot Pack: Use for firm berries. Wash fruit; drain. Add ½ cup sugar per quart. Bring to boiling in covered pan. Shake pan to prevent sticking. Pack hot fruit into hot jars, leaving ½-inch headspace. Adjust lids. Process.	10	15
Cherries *(Allow 2 to 2½ pounds unpitted cherries for each quart)*	*Raw Pack:* Prepare syrup; keep hot but not boiling. Wash and stem; pit, if desired. Fill hot jars, leaving ½-inch headspace. Bring syrup to boiling. Cover fruit with boiling syrup, leaving ½-inch headspace. Adjust lids. Process.	20	25
	Hot Pack: Wash and stem; pit, if desired. Add ½ cup sugar to each quart. Add a little water only to unpitted cherries. Cover; bring to boiling. Pack hot cherries into hot jars, leaving ½-inch headspace. Adjust lids. Process.	10	15

Fruit	Preparation of Fruit	Water bath in minutes (pints)	Water bath in minutes (quarts)
Grapefruit *(Allow 9 medium for 4 pints)*	*Raw Pack:* Peel grapefruit; remove all membrane. Section fruit over bowl to catch juice. Drain; reserve 1 cup juice. Pack fruit into hot jars; leave ½-inch headspace. Bring reserved juice and ½ cup sugar to a boil. Cover fruit in jars, leaving ½-inch headspace. Adjust lids. Process.	20	20
Mangoes *(Allow 3 large mangoes for 3 pints)*	*Raw Pack:* Prepare light syrup; keep hot but not boiling. Wash fruit; peel. With sharp knife slice fruit away from stone in ¼-inch slices. Place slices in hot jars, leaving ½-inch headspace. Bring syrup to boiling; cover fruit with boiling syrup, leaving ½-inch headspace. Adjust lids. Process.	15	20
Peaches-Pears *(Allow 2 to 3 pounds for each quart)*	*Raw Pack:* Prepare light or medium syrup; keep hot but not boiling. Wash fruit and peel. Dip peaches in boiling water, then in cold water for easier peeling. Halve and pit peaches and core pears. Prepare enough to fill one jar at a time. While preparing fruit, add color keeper (see tip, page 19). Pack into hot jars, leaving ½-inch headspace. Bring syrup to boiling. Cover fruit with syrup, leaving ½-inch headspace. Adjust lids. Repeat with remaining fruit. Process. *Hot Pack:* Prepare as above, but heat fruit through in syrup. Pack hot fruit into hot jars, leaving ½-inch headspace. Cover with boiling syrup, leaving ½-inch headspace. Adjust lids. Process in boiling water bath.	25 20	30 25
Plums *(Allow 1½ to 2½ pounds for each quart)*	*Raw Pack:* Prepare medium syrup; keep hot but not boiling. Wash and drain plums. Prick skins if canning plums whole. (This does not prevent skins from splitting, but helps to prevent skins from bursting.) Halve and pit freestone plums, if desired. Pack plums into hot jars, leaving ½-inch headspace. Bring syrup to boiling. Cover with boiling syrup, leaving ½-inch headspace. Adjust lids. Process. *Hot Pack:* Prepare as above, but bring plums to boiling in syrup. Pack hot plums into hot jars, leaving ½-inch headspace. Bring syrup to boiling. Cover with boiling syrup, leaving ½-inch headspace. Adjust lids. Process.	20 20	25 25
Rhubarb *(Allow 1 to 2 pounds for each quart)*	*Raw Pack:* Prepare light syrup; keep hot but not boiling. Wash and cut rhubarb stalks into ½-inch pieces. Pack rhubarb into hot jars, leaving ½-inch headspace. Bring syrup to boiling. Cover rhubarb with boiling syrup, leaving ½-inch headspace. Adjust lids. Process. *Hot Pack:* Prepare as above, but heat rhubarb through in syrup. Pack hot rhubarb into hot jars, leaving ½-inch headspace. Bring syrup to boiling. Cover with boiling syrup, leaving ½-inch headspace. Adjust lids. Process.	10 10	10 10
Fruit Juices	Wash fruit. Pit, if desired; crush. Heat to simmering; strain through cheesecloth bag. Add sugar (1 cup per gallon of juice). Heat to simmering. Pour hot juice into hot jars, leaving ½-inch headspace. Adjust lids. Process.	5	5

APPLE-CHERRY JUICE

    3 pounds apples
    4 cups tart red cherries
    3 cups water
    ½ cup sugar
        Few drops red food coloring

Thoroughly wash and core apples. Wash and pit cherries. Grind apples and cherries through food chopper, using a fine blade. In a 4- to 6-quart kettle or Dutch oven bring fruit and water to boiling, stirring occasionally. Reduce heat; cook slowly about 10 minutes. Strain through clean muslin or several thicknesses of cheesecloth. Let fruit juice stand 1 to 2 hours to let sediment settle.

Carefully pour off juice. Add sugar and food coloring to juice and heat through. Pour hot juice into hot jars, leaving ½-inch headspace. Adjust lids. Process in boiling water bath (pints) 15 minutes. Makes 3 pints.

Spicy Pear Compote *(page 52) is the delicious result of combining* Whole Cranberry Sauce *(page 23) and luscious home-canned* Pears *(page 21).*

PINEAPPLE-GRAPEFRUIT JUICE

    2 large pineapples
    6 large grapefruit

Remove crowns from pineapples; thoroughly wash and peel. Remove pineapple eyes; quarter and cut out core. Grind pineapple through food chopper, using fine blade. In medium saucepan bring pineapple to boiling; reduce heat and simmer 10 minutes. Strain through clean muslin; measure 3 cups juice. Cut grapefruit in half. Extract and strain juice; measure 6 cups. Combine juices. Bring to boiling. Pour hot juice into hot jars, leaving ½-inch headspace. Adjust lids. Process in boiling water bath (pints and quarts) 20 minutes. Makes 4 pints.

APPLE JUICE

Wash, core, and cut up 10 pounds apples. Grind through food chopper, using coarsest blade. In 8- to 10-quart kettle or Dutch oven combine apples and 1 cup water; cook and stir till bubbly. Strain through clean muslin or several thicknesses of cheesecloth. When cool, squeeze to extract remaining juice. Strain juice again. Add sugar to taste. Heat juice and pour into hot jars, leaving ½-inch headspace. Adjust lids. Process in boiling water bath (pints or quarts) 10 minutes. Makes 4 pints.

GRAPE JUICE CONCENTRATE

    6 pounds Concord grapes
    1½ cups sugar

Wash grapes; remove from stems. Measure 14 cups grapes. Combine grapes and 2 cups water in 6-quart kettle; cover. Heat to boiling; cook slowly until very tender, about 30 minutes. Remove from heat; strain through muslin or cheesecloth. Let juice stand 24 hours in refrigerator. Strain again. Combine grape juice and sugar in large kettle; heat to boiling. Pour hot juice into hot jars, leaving ½-inch headspace. Adjust lids. Process in boiling water bath (pints) 10 minutes. Makes 3 pints.

Before serving: Dilute grape juice concentrate with water to taste; chill thoroughly.

Sugar-free canning

All fruits and fruit juices may be canned successfully without sugar syrup or sweetening. Sugar helps to retain color and adds sweetness, but it is not necessary to prevent spoilage. To can without sugar, cook fruit till boiling and pack it into hot jars. Cover with boiling fruit juice, if possible, or add boiling water. Process in a water-bath canner.

APRICOT NECTAR

2 pounds apricots
5 cups water
1 cup sugar

Pit and slice apricots; measure 6 cups fruit. In 8- to 10-quart kettle or Dutch oven combine apricots and water. Cook till soft, 5 to 10 minutes. Press apricots through food mill. Measure about 7 cups purée; add sugar. Heat and stir till sugar is dissolved and mixture is heated through. Pour hot juice into hot jars, leaving ½-inch headspace. Adjust lids. Process in boiling water bath (pints or quarts) 10 minutes. Makes 4 pints.
Before serving: Chill and shake well.

BANANA BUTTER

3½ pounds ripe bananas
3 cups sugar
½ cup lemon juice
½ cup finely chopped red maraschino cherries
1 teaspoon butter or margarine

Thoroughly mash bananas; measure 4 cups into 4- to 6-quart kettle or Dutch oven. Add sugar, lemon juice, cherries, and butter; mix well. Bring to hard rolling boil, stirring constantly. Reduce heat; simmer gently, uncovered, 20 minutes, stirring often. Pour into hot jars, leaving ½-inch headspace. Adjust lids. Process in boiling water bath (half-pints) 10 minutes. Makes 6 half-pints.

APRICOT-ORANGE BUTTER

2 pounds apricots
1½ cups sugar
¾ cup honey
3 tablespoons frozen orange juice concentrate, thawed

Pit and slice apricots; measure 6 cups. Cook apricots in ½ cup water, covered, till soft, 5 to 10 minutes. Press through food mill; measure 3 cups. In 4- to 6-quart kettle or Dutch oven combine apricot purée, sugar, and honey. Bring to full boil; reduce heat and simmer gently, stirring constantly, 12 to 15 minutes. Stir in orange juice concentrate. Pour into hot jars, leaving ½-inch headspace. Adjust lids. Process in boiling water bath (half-pints) 10 minutes. Makes 4 half-pints.

APPLE BUTTER

6 pounds tart apples
6 cups cider or apple juice
3 cups sugar
2 teaspoons ground cinnamon
½ teaspoon ground cloves

Core and quarter unpeeled apples. In 4- to 6-quart kettle or Dutch oven combine apples and cider. Cook till soft, about 30 minutes. Press through food mill. Boil gently 30 minutes; stir occasionally. Add sugar and spices. Cook and stir over low heat till sugar dissolves. Boil gently, stirring frequently, till of desired thickness. Carefully ladle the hot butter into hot jars, leaving ½-inch headspace. Adjust lids. Process in boiling water bath (half-pints) 10 minutes. Makes 8 half-pints.

WHOLE CRANBERRY SAUCE

Combine 6¾ cups sugar and 6 cups water in an 8- to 10-quart kettle or Dutch oven; stir to dissolve sugar. Heat mixture to boiling; boil 5 minutes. Add 3 pounds (12 cups) fresh cranberries; cook till skins pop, about 5 minutes. Remove from heat. Pack hot cranberry sauce into hot jars, leaving ½-inch headspace. Adjust lids. Process in boiling water bath (pints) 5 minutes. Makes 6 pints.

ROSY FRUIT COCKTAIL

The delicate pink color of this fruit cocktail (see photo, page 18) comes from dark sweet cherries—

5¼ cups Light or Medium Syrup (see page 20)
1 2-pound pineapple
3 pounds peaches
3 pounds pears
1 pound dark sweet cherries
1 pound seedless green grapes
   Ascorbic acid color keeper

Prepare syrup; keep hot but not boiling. Wash pineapple, peaches, pears, dark sweet cherries, and seedless grapes. Remove crown from pineapple. Peel and cut pineapple in tidbits, removing eyes and center core. Measure 3 cups. Peel and pit peaches; cut in cubes and measure 8½ cups peaches. Peel and core pears; cut in cubes and measure 6½ cups pears. While preparing peaches and pears, add color keeper (see tip, page 19). Halve and pit dark sweet cherries; measure 2½ cups fruit. Stem seedless green grapes; measure 3 cups.

In 4- to 6-quart kettle or Dutch oven combine all fruit. Add hot syrup and bring to boiling. Pack hot fruit into hot jars, leaving ½-inch headspace. Cover fruit with boiling syrup, leaving ½-inch headspace. Adjust lids. Process in boiling water bath (pints and quarts) 30 minutes. Makes 9 pints.

STRAWBERRY-RHUBARB SAUCE

Enjoy this springtime duo all winter long—

1½ pounds rhubarb
4 cups strawberries
1 to 1½ cups sugar
¼ cup water
2 teaspoons lemon juice

Thoroughly wash rhubarb and strawberries. Cut rhubarb into 1-inch pieces. Remove hulls from strawberries; halve large berries. In 4- to 6-quart kettle or Dutch oven combine rhubarb, strawberries, sugar, water, and lemon juice. Bring fruit to boiling; boil ½ minute.

Pack hot fruit and syrup into hot jars, leaving ½-inch headspace. Adjust lids. Process in boiling water bath (half-pints and pints) 15 minutes. Makes 7 half-pints.

MINTED PEARS

Green crème de menthe adds an interesting color and flavor to these pears (pictured on page 18)—

4¾ cups Very Light Syrup (see page 20)
7 pounds pears
   Ascorbic acid color keeper
⅔ cup green crème de menthe
   Green food coloring (optional)

Prepare syrup; keep hot but not boiling. Wash, peel, halve, and core pears. While preparing fruit, add color keeper (see tip, page 19). In 4- to 6-quart kettle or Dutch oven stir crème de menthe into syrup. Add green food coloring, if desired. Add pears; heat 2 to 3 minutes. Pack hot pears into hot jars, leaving ½-inch headspace. Cover with hot syrup, leaving ½-inch headspace. Adjust lids. Process in boiling water bath (pints) 25 minutes; (quarts) 30 minutes. Makes 7 pints.

PINEAPPLE SPEARS

These attractive spears are pictured on page 7—

Prepare Medium Syrup (see page 20); keep hot but not boiling. Wash two 4½-pound pineapples thoroughly. Remove crowns. Peel pineapples and remove eyes. Quarter and remove core. Cut fruit in spears that are ½-inch shorter than the height of the pint jars.

In 4- to 6-quart kettle or Dutch oven bring spears and syrup to boiling. Boil about 7 minutes. Pack hot fruit into hot pint jars. Cover with boiling syrup, leaving ½-inch headspace. Adjust lids. Process in boiling water bath (pints) 30 minutes. Makes 3 pints.

MELON BALLS

4¾ cups Very Light Syrup (see page 20)
4 cups cantaloupe balls
4 cups honeydew balls
   Lime juice

Prepare syrup; keep hot but not boiling. Pack melon balls into hot jars, leaving ½-inch headspace. Add ½ teaspoon lime juice and syrup to each half-pint, leaving ½-inch headspace. Adjust lids. Process in boiling water bath (half-pints) 20 minutes. Makes 7 half-pints.

FRUIT BOWL

4¾ cups Very Light Syrup or Light Syrup
    (see page 20)
2 3-pound pineapples
2 pounds seedless green grapes
2 pounds fully ripe apricots
    Ascorbic acid color keeper

Prepare syrup; keep hot but not boiling. Wash pineapples. Remove crowns. Slice and peel pineapples; remove eyes and core from each slice. Cut pineapple into chunks. Wash and drain grapes. Remove stems. Wash and drain apricots; halve and pit. While preparing apricots, add color keeper (see tip, page 19).

   Simmer pineapple chunks in hot syrup till tender, 5 to 10 minutes. Add apricots and grapes; simmer fruit till heated through, about 5 minutes. Pack hot fruit into hot jars, leaving 1-inch headspace. Cover with boiling syrup, leaving ½-inch headspace. Adjust lids. Process in boiling water bath (pints) 20 minutes; (quarts) 25 minutes. Makes 8 pints.

   Before serving: If desired, to each pint add ¼ cup maraschino cherry halves; chill.

APPLE PIE FILLING

4½ cups sugar
1 cup cornstarch
2 teaspoons ground cinnamon
¼ teaspoon ground nutmeg
3 tablespoons lemon juice
2 or 3 drops yellow food coloring
5½ to 6 pounds tart apples, peeled,
    cored, and sliced

In large saucepan blend first 4 ingredients and 1 teaspoon salt. Stir in 10 cups water; cook and stir till thickened and bubbly. Add lemon juice and food coloring. Pack apples into hot jars, leaving 1-inch headspace. Fill with hot syrup, leaving ½-inch headspace. (Use spatula to help distribute syrup.) Adjust lids. Process in boiling water bath (pints) 15 minutes; (quarts) 20 minutes. Makes 6 quarts.

   Before serving: Prepare pastry for a 2-crust 8- or 9-inch pie. Line pie plate with pastry; add 1 quart apple pie filling. Adjust top crust, cutting slits for escape of steam; seal. Bake at 400° for 50 minutes.

SPICED PEACHES

5 cups sugar
2 cups water
1 cup vinegar
12 inches stick cinnamon, broken
2 teaspoons whole cloves
2½ pounds peaches

In 4- to 6-quart kettle or Dutch oven combine sugar, water, vinegar, cinnamon, and whole cloves. Heat syrup to boiling; keep hot but not boiling. Wash peaches; peel, halve, and pit. To prevent discoloration, add the peach halves to syrup as soon as they are cut. Heat peaches in hot syrup 5 minutes. Pack fruit and syrup into hot jars, leaving ½-inch headspace. Adjust lids. Process in boiling water bath (pints) 20 minutes. Makes 3 pints.

LEMON SYRUP

1 large lemon
3 cups water
4 cups sugar
2 tablespoons citric acid

Halve lemon and squeeze juice. Quarter lemon halves and scrape away white membrane. In 4- to 6-quart kettle or Dutch oven heat lemon peel, juice, and water to boiling. Simmer 10 minutes; strain. Combine strained liquid, sugar, and citric acid; heat to boiling. Simmer 5 minutes. Pour hot syrup into hot jars, leaving ½-inch headspace. Adjust lids. Process in boiling water bath (half-pints and pints) 10 minutes. Makes 5 half-pints.

STRAWBERRY SYRUP

Wash and hull 6 pints strawberries. Put strawberries in blender container to mash; blend thoroughly. In 8- to 10-quart kettle or Dutch oven combine strawberries and 7 cups sugar. Heat to full boil; reduce heat. Boil gently 10 minutes. Strain juice through jelly bag; drain several hours or overnight. Return juice to kettle and heat. Pour hot syrup into hot jars, leaving ½-inch headspace. Adjust lids. Process in boiling water bath (half-pints) 10 minutes. Makes 5 to 6 half-pints.

CANNED TOMATOES

>   **15 pounds tomatoes**
>   **Lemon juice**
>   **Salt**

Use firm, fully ripe tomatoes of about the same size. To loosen skins, dip tomatoes in boiling water ½ minute. Water must be kept at or near boiling point. Then, dip tomatoes quickly into cold water before peeling.

Cut out stem ends and cores, if present. Pack small or medium tomatoes whole, but cut large tomatoes in quarters or eighths. Use a small spoon to scrape out the excess seeds, if desired. Follow directions below for either raw or hot pack. Makes 6 quarts.

Raw Pack: Pack tomatoes in hot jars, pressing gently to fill spaces; leave ½-inch headspace. Add no water. Add 1 teaspoon lemon juice to each quart or ½ teaspoon to each pint (see tip box). Add ½ teaspoon salt to each quart or ¼ teaspoon to each pint. Adjust lids. Process in boiling water bath (pints) 35 minutes; (quarts) 45 minutes.

Hot Pack: In 8- to 10-quart kettle or Dutch oven bring tomatoes to boiling, stirring constantly but gently. Pack hot tomatoes into hot jars; leave ½-inch headspace. Add 1 teaspoon lemon juice to each quart or ½ teaspoon to each pint (see tip box). Add ½ teaspoon salt to each quart or ¼ teaspoon to each pint. Adjust lids. Process in boiling water bath (pints and quarts) 10 minutes.

TOMATO JUICE

Thoroughly wash 9 pounds tomatoes. Remove stem ends and cores, if present; cut tomatoes in pieces. Measure about 20 cups of tomatoes. In 8- to 10-quart kettle or Dutch oven slowly cook the tomatoes, covered, until soft, about 15 minutes. Stir often to prevent sticking.

Press through food mill or sieve to extract juice; measure 12 cups. Return tomato juice to kettle and bring to a boil. Stir in 1 tablespoon lemon juice (see tip box). Pour hot tomato juice into hot jars, leaving ½-inch headspace. Add ¼ teaspoon salt to each pint or ½ teaspoon to each quart. Adjust lids. Process in boiling water bath (pints) 10 minutes; (quarts) 15 minutes. Makes 6 pints.

TOMATO JUICE COCKTAIL

>   **8 pounds tomatoes**
>   **1 cup chopped celery**
>   **½ cup chopped onion**
>   **¼ cup lemon juice**
>   **1 tablespoon sugar**
>   **2 teaspoons salt**
>   **2 teaspoons prepared horseradish**
>   **2 teaspoons Worcestershire sauce**
>   **¼ teaspoon bottled hot pepper sauce**

Wash tomatoes and remove stem ends and cores, if present. Cut up tomatoes. Measure 19 cups. In 8- to 10-quart kettle or Dutch oven combine tomatoes, celery, and onion. Cover and cook slowly until tomatoes are soft, about 15 minutes. Stir often. Press tomatoes through food mill to extract juice; measure 12 cups.

Boil juice gently, uncovered, about 30 minutes, stirring often. Measure 9½ to 10 cups juice. Add lemon juice, sugar, salt, horseradish, Worcestershire sauce, and bottled hot pepper sauce; simmer 10 minutes. Pour hot juice into hot jars, leaving ½-inch headspace. Adjust lids. Process in boiling water bath (pints) 10 minutes. Makes 5 pints.

CHILI SAUCE

>   **12 to 14 pounds tomatoes**
>   **4 cups chopped celery**
>   **2½ cups ground onion**
>   **2½ cups ground green pepper**
>   **6 inches stick cinnamon**
>   **4½ cups packed brown sugar**
>   **4 cups cider vinegar**
>   **¼ cup salt**
>   **1 tablespoon dry mustard**
>   **1½ teaspoons ground cloves**

Wash, peel, remove stem ends and cores, and quarter tomatoes into 8- to 10-quart kettle or Dutch oven. Cook 15 minutes; drain off 6 cups tomato juice (use for cooking or drinking). Add celery, onion, and green pepper; simmer 1½ hours. Tie stick cinnamon in cloth; add to mixture. Add brown sugar, vinegar, salt, mustard, and cloves. Cook mixture 1½ hours. Remove spice bag. Pour into hot jars, leaving ½-inch headspace. Adjust lids. Process in boiling water bath (pints) 5 minutes. Makes 9 pints.

Adding lemon juice to tomatoes

Several new tomato varieties are relatively low in acid content. This may interfere with the tomatoes' keeping quality when processed in a boiling water bath. Because you may not know the acidity of the tomatoes you are canning, add ½ teaspoon lemon juice to each pint jar or 1 teaspoon per quart. This will ensure a correct acid level without affecting the flavor.

BEST TOMATO CATSUP

8 pounds tomatoes
1 medium onion, chopped
¼ teaspoon cayenne
1 cup sugar
1 cup white vinegar
1½ teaspoons whole cloves
1½ inches stick cinnamon, broken
1 teaspoon celery seed
4 teaspoons salt

Wash, peel, remove stem ends and cores, and quarter tomatoes. Let tomatoes stand in colander to drain off excess liquid. In 8- to 10-quart kettle or Dutch oven mix tomatoes, onion, and cayenne. Bring to boiling; cook until tomatoes are soft, about 15 minutes, stirring occasionally. Put tomatoes through food mill or a coarse sieve; press to extract juice. Add sugar to tomato juice and return to kettle. Bring to a boil; then simmer briskly 1½ to 2 hours or till mixture is reduced by half (measure depth with ruler at start and end).

Meanwhile, in small saucepan combine white vinegar, whole cloves, stick cinnamon, and celery seed. Cover; bring vinegar mixture to boiling. Remove from heat; let stand.

Strain spiced vinegar mixture into tomato sauce. Discard the spices. Add salt to mixture; simmer till of desired consistency, about 30 minutes. Stir the tomato catsup often to prevent sticking.

Pour hot catsup into hot jars, leaving ½-inch headspace. Adjust lids. Process in boiling water bath (pints) 5 minutes. Makes 2 pints.

TOMATO SAUCE

8 pounds tomatoes
1 cup chopped green pepper
1 medium onion, chopped
1 teaspoon celery seed
¼ teaspoon cayenne
2 tablespoons white vinegar
1 tablespoon sugar
1 teaspoon salt

Wash, remove stem ends and cores, and quarter tomatoes. Let tomatoes stand in colander to drain off excess liquid. In 8- to 10-quart kettle or Dutch oven combine tomatoes, green pepper, chopped onion, celery seed, and cayenne. Bring to a boil; cook 40 to 45 minutes, stirring occasionally. Put tomato pulp through food mill or a coarse sieve. Add white vinegar, sugar, and salt to the tomato purée. Return the purée to the kettle.

Bring to a boil; simmer till of desired consistency, 30 minutes. Stir sauce often. Pour hot tomato sauce into hot jars, leaving ½-inch headspace. Adjust lids. Process in boiling water bath (pints) 10 minutes. Makes 2 pints.

TOMATO-MUSHROOM SAUCE

8 pounds tomatoes
1 teaspoon celery seed
1 teaspoon mustard seed
¼ teaspoon cayenne
2 cups chopped fresh mushrooms
2 tablespoons white vinegar
1 tablespoon sugar
1 teaspoon salt

Wash, remove stem ends and cores, and quarter tomatoes. Let tomatoes stand in colander to drain off excess liquid. In 8- to 10-quart kettle or Dutch oven combine tomatoes, celery seed, mustard seed, and cayenne. Bring to a boil; cook 30 minutes, stirring occasionally.

Put tomato pulp through food mill or coarse sieve. Add chopped mushrooms, white vinegar, sugar, and salt to tomato purée. Return the purée to kettle. Bring to a boil; simmer till of desired consistency, 45 minutes. Stir often. Pour hot sauce into hot jars; leave ½-inch headspace. Adjust lids. Process in boiling water bath (pints) 30 minutes. Makes 2 pints.

LOW-ACID VEGETABLES

Despite their differences in shape, color, and flavor, vegetables have one thing in common from the home canner's point of view: With the practical exception of tomatoes, they do not have natural acidity. This means that you must can them in a pressure canner at 10 pounds pressure. This rule applies to all low-acid vegetables except those made into pickles, relishes, and sauerkraut. These foods are prepared with vinegar and/or brine to have a preservative effect on the product. The vinegar also boosts the amount of acidity. Only then is water bath processing adequate for safety.

Getting Vegetables Ready

To achieve good results when canning vegetables, you must work with produce that is fresh, young, and tender. To preserve this quality, minimize the time between picking and canning. Many experienced home canners say, "no more than two hours from the time the vegetable is picked till it goes into the canner." This timetable is realistic for the home gardener, and it is a good target for those whose source of vegetables is a roadside stand or a nearby supermarket.

Assembling jars, lids, pressure canner, and miscellaneous kitchen equipment before picking or buying the vegetables enables you to work quickly with the produce once you have it in hand. Doing small batches is another means of maintaining quality.

Thorough washing is important, but don't let vegetables stand in water. Lift them up and down in the water to help remove soil. Each time the water is changed, lift the vegetables out of the water. Draining off the water lets the dirt resettle on the food.

Sweet corn all winter long

← *Capture the goodness of your home-grown sweet corn by canning it either whole-kernel or cream-style for wintertime enjoyment. Serve it piping hot with butter or use it in* Swiss Corn Bake *(page 50).*

Headspace for starchy vegetables

Vegetables with a high starch content, such as potatoes, corn, peas, and lima beans, expand while being processed in the pressure canner. Always be sure to allow 1-inch headspace when packing these vegetables into the jars.

Packing the Jars

After the vegetables have been cleaned, peeled, or cut up as directed, it is time to fill the jars. For hot-pack foods, use the liquid in which the vegetables were cooked unless it is murky, gritty, or generally unattractive. This liquid contains any water-soluble nutrients that came out of the foods. Likewise, in raw-pack canning, boil the final soaking water to use as liquid for filling the jars to preserve the same nutrients. Otherwise, use fresh, boiling water for filling jars.

Complete step-by-step directions and photographs showing how to fill the jars begin on page 11. Be sure to allow the right amount of headspace. As is indicated in the tip box, this is most important for starchy vegetables.

Pressure Processing

All low-acid vegetables must be processed in a pressure canner for an adequate period of time to destroy the heat-resistant bacteria, which could cause food poisoning. This statement, along with its corollary concerning boiling the vegetables 10 to 15 minutes before tasting or serving, is so important that it is repeated at intervals throughout this book. Detailed information on how to use a pressure canner begins on page 14. It covers how to bring up the pressure, maintain it, and tell when it is back to normal. If you need an altitude correction, there are instructions in a tip box on page 15.

Canning Vegetables

Vegetable	Preparation of Vegetables	Pressure canner minutes at 10 lbs. (pints)	Pressure canner minutes at 10 lbs. (quarts)
	Follow directions for raw pack or hot pack as indicated for each vegetable. Add ½ teaspoon salt for each quart or ¼ teaspoon salt for each pint.		
Asparagus *(Allow 2½ to 4½ pounds for each quart)*	*Raw Pack:* Thoroughly wash asparagus. Trim off scales and tough ends; cut in 1-inch pieces. Pack into hot jars; leave ½-inch headspace. Add salt. Cover with boiling water; leave ½-inch headspace. Adjust lids and process.	25	30
	Hot Pack: Prepare asparagus as above. Then, cover asparagus pieces with boiling water; boil 3 minutes. Pack hot asparagus into hot jars, leaving ½-inch headspace. Add salt. Cover with boiling cooking liquid, leaving ½-inch headspace. Adjust lids and process.	25	30
Beans Green and Wax *(Allow 1½ to 2½ pounds for each quart)*	*Raw Pack:* Thoroughly wash green or wax beans. Trim ends and cut beans in 1-inch pieces. Pack in hot jars; leave ½-inch headspace. Add salt. Cover beans with boiling water, leaving ½-inch headspace. Adjust lids and process.	20	25
	Hot Pack: Prepare beans as above. Then, cover green or wax beans with boiling water; boil 5 minutes. Pack hot beans into hot jars, leaving ½-inch headspace. Add salt. Cover hot green or wax beans with boiling cooking liquid, leaving ½-inch headspace. Adjust lids and process.	20	25
Beans Lima *(Allow 3 to 5 pounds for each quart)*	*Raw Pack:* Shell and wash young beans. Pack the lima beans into hot jars, leaving 1-inch headspace. Add salt. Cover with boiling water, leaving 1-inch headspace. Adjust lids and process.	40	50
	Hot Pack: Prepare lima beans as above. Then, cover with boiling water; bring to boiling. Pack hot beans loosely into hot jars, leaving 1-inch headspace. Add salt. Cover beans with boiling cooking liquid, leaving 1-inch headspace. Adjust lids and process.	40	50
Beets *(Allow 2 to 3½ pounds for each quart)*	Wash beets, leaving on root and 1 inch of the tops. Cover beets with boiling water and cook 15 minutes. Cool just enough to handle. Slip off skins from beets and trim. Slice beets. Pack hot beets into hot jars, leaving ½-inch headspace. Add salt. Cover with boiling water, leaving ½-inch headspace. Adjust lids and process.	30	35
Carrots *(Allow 2 to 3 pounds for each quart)*	*Raw Pack:* Thoroughly wash carrots. Peel, then slice or dice. Pack carrots tightly into hot jars, leaving ½-inch headspace. Add salt. Cover with boiling water, leaving ½-inch headspace. Adjust lids and process.	25	30
	Hot Pack: Wash, peel, and slice or dice carrots. Cover with boiling water and bring to a boil. Pack the hot carrots into hot jars, leaving ½-inch headspace. Add salt. Cover with boiling cooking liquid, leaving ½-inch headspace. Adjust lids and process.	25	30

Vegetable	Preparation of Vegetables	Pressure canner minutes at 10 lbs. (pints)	Pressure canner minutes at 10 lbs. (quarts)
Corn Whole Kernel *(Allow 3 to 6 pounds for each quart)*	*Raw Pack:* Cut corn from cob at ⅔'s depth; do not scrape cob. Pack corn loosely into hot jars, leaving 1-inch head-space. Add salt. Cover with boiling water, leaving 1-inch headspace. Adjust lids and process. *Hot Pack:* Prepare as above. Add 2 cups boiling water per 1 quart of corn; bring to a boil. Pack loosely. Add salt and boiling cooking liquid; leave 1-inch headspace.	55 55	85 85
Corn Cream-Style *(Allow 1½ to 3 pounds for each pint)*	*Raw Pack:* Cut corn from cob, cutting only about half the kernel; scrape cob. Follow directions above, except pack cream-style corn into hot pint jars, leaving 1-inch head-space. Fill jars with boiling water, leaving 1-inch headspace. *Hot Pack:* Cut corn from cob; scrape cob. Cover with boiling water; bring to a boil. Pack hot corn in hot pint jars. Leave 1-inch headspace. Adjust lids and process.	95 85	
Mushrooms *(Allow ¾ pound for each pint)*	Wash; trim stems. Slice or leave small mushrooms whole. Add color keeper (see tip, page 19); drain. Heat gently, covered, without liquid for 15 minutes. Pack hot into hot jars, leaving ½-inch headspace. Add salt. Cover with boiling water, leaving ½-inch headspace. Adjust lids and process.	30	
Peas Green *(Allow 3 to 6 pounds for each quart)*	*Raw Pack:* Shell; wash peas. Pack loosely, leaving 1-inch headspace. Add salt. Cover with boiling water, leaving 1-inch headspace. Adjust lids and process. *Hot Pack:* Prepare as above. Cover with boiling water; bring to a boil. Pack hot, leaving 1-inch headspace. Add salt. Cover with boiling water, leaving 1-inch headspace. Adjust lids; process.	40 40	40 40
Potatoes New white *(Allow 5 to 6 pounds per quart)*	Wash; cook in boiling water 10 minutes. Remove skins. Pack hot potatoes in hot jars, leaving 1-inch headspace. Add salt. Cover with boiling water, leaving 1-inch headspace. Adjust lids and process.	30	40
Potatoes Sweet *(Allow 2 to 3 pounds for each quart)*	*Dry Pack:* Wash; cook in boiling water 20 to 30 minutes. Remove skins; cut up. Pack hot, leaving 1-inch headspace. Add no liquid or salt. Adjust lids and process. *Wet Pack:* Wash; boil till skins slip off easily. Remove skins; cut in pieces. Pack hot; leave 1-inch headspace. Add salt. Cover with boiling water; leave 1-inch headspace. Adjust lids.	65 55	95 90
Pumpkin or Winter Squash *(Allow 1½ to 3 pounds for each quart)*	Wash; remove seeds. Peel and cube. Barely cover with water; bring to a boil. Pack hot; add salt. Cover with boiling water, leaving ½-inch headspace. Adjust lids; process. *Mashed pumpkin or squash:* Wash; remove seeds. Peel and cut up. Steam till tender. Put through food mill. Heat through; stir to prevent sticking. Pack hot, leaving ½-inch headspace. Add no salt or liquid. Adjust lids; process.	55 65	90 80

SAUERKRAUT

Use 5 pounds fully matured cabbage. Wash, quarter, core, and finely shred cabbage. Sprinkle 3½ tablespoons salt over cabbage; mix well. Let stand 30 to 60 minutes. Firmly pack into room-temperature jars, leaving a 2-inch headspace. Fill with cold water, leaving ½-inch headspace. Adjust lids, screwing band tight. Place jars on jelly-roll pan to catch brine that overflows during fermentation and curing. Keep cabbage covered with brine. If necessary, open jars and add more brine made by dissolving 1½ tablespoons salt in 1 quart water.

Sauerkraut is cured and ready to can in 6 to 8 weeks. Clean rims of jars, replacing lids if sealer appears damaged; screw band tight. Set jars in water bath canner filled with cold water. Water should extend 2 inches above jars. Bring water slowly to boiling. Process sauerkraut (pints or quarts) 30 minutes. Makes 7 pints.

ZUCCHINI-VEGETABLE COMBO

2 pounds unpeeled zucchini, sliced
2 pounds tomatoes, peeled, stem ends
**   and cores removed, and cut up**
1 cup chopped onion
1 cup chopped green pepper

In 4- to 6-quart kettle or Dutch oven combine zucchini, tomatoes, onion, green pepper, and 2½ cups water. Bring to boiling; boil 2 to 3 minutes. Pack hot vegetables into hot pint jars, leaving ½-inch headspace. Add ½ teaspoon salt per pint. Cover with boiling vegetable liquid, leaving ½-inch headspace. Adjust lids. Process in pressure canner at 10 pounds (pints or quarts) 40 minutes. Makes 8 pints.

Salt-free canning

All meats, poultry, seafoods, and low-acid vegetables may be canned successfully without adding salt. Salt is used only as a seasoning. The amounts used in canning are too small to have any preservative effect.

BEETS WITH PINEAPPLE

2 pounds beets
2 cups water
¾ cup packed brown sugar
2 cups fresh pineapple tidbits
Lemon juice
Salt

Wash beets, leaving on root and 1 inch of tops. Cover with boiling water; simmer 15 minutes. Slip off skins and trim; slice beets (about 5 cups). In 4- to 6-quart kettle or Dutch oven combine water and brown sugar; stir till sugar dissolves. Simmer pineapple in syrup for 5 minutes. Add beets and heat through. Pack hot beet slices and pineapple tidbits into hot jars, leaving ½-inch headspace. Add 1 teaspoon lemon juice and ¼ teaspoon salt to each pint. Cover with boiling syrup, leaving ½-inch headspace. Adjust lids. Process in pressure canner at 10 pounds pressure (pints) 30 minutes; (quarts) 40 minutes. Makes 4 pints.

Before serving: In saucepan boil beets with pineapple at least 10 minutes *before* tasting or using. For each pint, combine 2 teaspoons cornstarch and 1 tablespoon cold water. Stir into beet mixture with 1 tablespoon butter. Cook and stir till mixture thickens.

SUCCOTASH

4 cups shelled lima beans
6 to 8 medium ears sweet corn, cut
**   from cob**
4 cups water
Salt

Wash and drain beans. Combine beans and corn in kettle; add water. Bring to boiling; cook 5 minutes. Pack hot vegetables loosely into hot jars, leaving 1-inch headspace. Add ¼ teaspoon salt per pint. Pour in boiling cooking liquid, leaving 1-inch headspace. Adjust lids. Process in pressure canner at 10 pounds pressure (pints) 55 minutes; (quarts) 85 minutes. Makes 4 pints.

Before serving: Boil these vegetables 20 minutes *before* tasting or using. If desired, add ½ cup light cream and 2 tablespoons butter or margarine to each pint of succotash; or add 1 tablespoon chopped canned pimiento.

Looking for an interesting way to serve your home-canned sauerkraut?
Use it as the basis for the peppy relish in these Kraut Relish Stack-Ups
(page 49). Save any extra relish to pass with cold roast beef or ham.

HERBED GREEN BEANS

 3 pounds green beans
1½ cups chopped onion
 1 cup chopped celery
 1 clove garlic, minced
 ¼ teaspoon dried rosemary, crushed
 ¼ teaspoon dried basil, crushed

Wash and drain green beans. Trim ends and cut in 1-inch pieces; measure 12 cups. In 4- to 6-quart kettle or Dutch oven simmer beans in boiling water to cover for 5 minutes; drain. Combine green beans, onion, celery, garlic, rosemary, and basil. Pack mixture into hot jars, leaving ½-inch headspace. Cover with boiling water, leaving ½-inch headspace. Add ¼ teaspoon salt per pint. Adjust lids. Process in pressure canner at 10 pounds pressure (pints) 20 minutes. Makes 6 pints.

Before serving: Boil at least 10 minutes *before* tasting or using; drain. Add 1 tablespoon butter or margarine to each pint, if desired.

MIXED VEGETABLES

1½ pounds carrots
 10 to 11 medium ears sweet corn
1½ pounds green beans
 4 cups shelled lima beans

Thoroughly wash carrots. Peel and chop carrots. Remove corn husks and silks from sweet corn ears. Rinse and cut sweet corn from cobs. Wash green beans; drain. Trim ends and cut green beans in 1-inch pieces. Wash lima beans; drain. In 8- to 10-quart kettle or Dutch oven cover carrots, sweet corn, green beans, and lima beans with boiling water. Bring mixed vegetables to a boil.

Keep vegetables at boiling temperature; pack hot mixed vegetables into hot jars, leaving 1-inch headspace. Add ½ teaspoon salt per pint. Cover mixed vegetables with boiling cooking liquid, leaving 1-inch headspace. Adjust lids. Process in pressure canner at 10 pounds (pints) 55 minutes. Makes 11 pints.

BEANS IN TOMATO SAUCE

     2 pounds dry navy beans (4 cups)
     3 quarts cold water
     3 cups tomato juice
     1 6-ounce can tomato paste
     ½ cup chopped onion
     ¼ cup chopped green pepper
     1 tablespoon Worcestershire sauce
     1 tablespoon sugar
     ½ teaspoon salt
       Few drops bottled hot pepper sauce
     2 teaspoons salt
     ¼ pound salt pork, cut in pieces

Rinse beans; add to 3 quarts cold water in 8- to 10-quart kettle or Dutch oven. Bring to boiling; simmer 2 minutes. Remove from heat; cover and let navy beans stand 1 hour.

Meanwhile, in large saucepan combine tomato juice, tomato paste, onion, green pepper, Worcestershire sauce, sugar, the ½ teaspoon salt, and hot pepper sauce. Cover and bring to boiling. Reduce heat; simmer 5 to 10 minutes.

Add the 2 teaspoons salt to beans and soaking water; cover and bring to boiling. Drain. Add salt pork to drained beans. Pack hot mixture into hot jars, filling jars ¾ full. Fill with boiling tomato sauce, leaving 1-inch headspace. Adjust lids. Process in pressure canner at 10 pounds pressure (pints) 80 minutes; (quarts) 100 minutes. Makes 6 pints.

THREE-BEAN COMBO

     1½ pounds green beans
     1½ pounds wax beans
     4 cups shelled lima beans
       Salt

Wash green beans and wax beans; drain. Trim ends and cut green and wax beans in 1-inch pieces. Wash shelled limas; drain. In 8- to 10-quart kettle or Dutch oven combine green beans, wax beans, and limas. Cover with boiling water; bring to boiling. Cook 5 minutes.

Pack hot beans into hot jars, leaving 1-inch headspace. Add ½ teaspoon salt per pint. Cover with boiling cooking liquid, leaving 1-inch headspace. Adjust lids. Process in pressure canner at 10 pounds pressure (pints) 40 minutes; (quarts) 50 minutes. Makes 7 pints.

BOSTON-STYLE BEANS

     2 pounds dry navy beans (4 cups)
     3 quarts cold water
     2 teaspoons salt
     ⅓ cup molasses
     ⅓ cup packed brown sugar
     2 tablespoons vinegar
     1 teaspoon dry mustard
     ½ teaspoon salt
     ¼ pound salt pork, cut in pieces

Rinse beans; add to 3 quarts cold water in 8- to 10-quart kettle or Dutch oven. Bring to boiling; simmer 2 minutes. Remove from heat; cover and let navy beans stand 1 hour.

Add the 2 teaspoons salt to beans and soaking water; cover and bring to boiling. Drain, reserving 3 cups of the liquid. In large saucepan combine reserved soaking liquid, molasses, brown sugar, vinegar, dry mustard, and the ½ teaspoon salt. Cover and bring to boiling; simmer 5 to 10 minutes. Keep sauce hot.

Add salt pork to drained beans. Pack hot mixture into hot jars, filling jars ¾ full. Fill with hot molasses sauce; leave 1-inch headspace. Adjust lids. Process in pressure canner at 10 pounds pressure (pints) 80 minutes; (quarts) 100 minutes. Makes 6 pints.

OKRA CREOLE

     4 pounds tomatoes
     1½ pounds okra
     1 cup chopped onion
     1 teaspoon salt
     ¼ teaspoon pepper

Use large, firm, fully ripe tomatoes. Wash and peel tomatoes. To loosen skins, dip in boiling water ½ minute; dip quickly in cold water. Remove stem ends and cores. Quarter tomatoes. After quartering, use a small spoon to scrape out excess tomato seeds, if desired. Wash okra; trim stem ends and cut in ½-inch slices. In 4- to 6-quart kettle or Dutch oven combine tomatoes, okra, chopped onion, salt, and pepper. Boil vegetables 3 minutes.

Pack hot vegetables into hot pint jars, leaving ½-inch headspace. Adjust lids. Process in pressure canner at 10 pounds pressure (pints) 30 minutes. Makes 5 pints.

Boil canned vegetables

Before tasting or using home-canned vegetables, boil, uncovered, at least 10 minutes (20 minutes for corn or spinach). Add water to prevent sticking.

PEAS AND ONIONS

6 pounds unshelled green peas
1½ pounds pearl onions

Shell and wash peas; measure 8 cups. Wash and peel onions; measure 3 cups. Cover peas and onions with boiling water; boil 5 minutes.

Pack hot peas and onions loosely into hot jars, leaving 1-inch headspace. Add ½ teaspoon salt to each pint; cover with boiling cooking liquid, leaving 1-inch headspace. Adjust lids. Process in pressure canner at 10 pounds (pints) 40 minutes. Makes 8 pints.

CORN AND CHEESE CHOWDER

5 to 6 medium ears sweet corn
3 cups boiling water
1 tablespoon instant chicken bouillon granules
4 cups diced, peeled potatoes
1½ cups sliced onion
1 cup chopped celery
¼ teaspoon pepper

Remove husks and silks from corn. Rinse and cut corn from cob, cutting only about half the kernel; scrape cob. Measure 4 cups of this cream-style corn. In 4- to 6-quart kettle or Dutch oven combine corn, boiling water, and bouillon granules. Bring corn to boiling; boil 3 minutes. Add potatoes, onion, celery, and pepper; heat through. Ladle hot soup into hot jars, leaving 1-inch headspace. Adjust lids. Process in pressure canner at 10 pounds pressure (pints) 85 minutes. Makes 5 pints.

Before serving: Boil 1 pint of chowder 10 minutes *before* tasting or using it. Reduce heat; add ½ cup milk and ¼ cup shredded sharp process American cheese. Stir to melt cheese; heat through.

VEGETABLE SOUP

2 cups chopped, peeled tomatoes
3 cups water
4 teaspoons instant beef bouillon granules
1 tablespoon Worcestershire sauce
½ teaspoon chili powder
3 cups cubed, peeled potatoes
3 cups sliced carrots
2½ cups cut green beans
2 cups corn cut from cob
1 cup chopped celery
½ cup chopped onion

In 4- to 6-quart kettle or Dutch oven combine tomatoes, water, bouillon, Worcestershire, chili powder, and 2 teaspoons salt; heat through. Add vegetables to soup mixture; boil 5 minutes. Pour hot soup into hot jars, leaving 1-inch headspace. Adjust lids. Process in pressure canner at 10 pounds (pints) 55 minutes; (quarts) 85 minutes. Makes 6 pints.

Before serving: Boil 1 pint vegetable soup 10 to 15 minutes *before* tasting or using; add ½ cup water to soup mixture.

CABBAGE BORSCH

5 pounds tomatoes
8 cups coarsely shredded cabbage
6 cups water
2 cups chopped onion
2 medium apples, peeled and cut in pieces
2 tablespoons instant beef bouillon granules
2 tablespoons sugar
2 tablespoons lemon juice
1 teaspoon salt
⅛ teaspoon pepper

Wash, peel, remove stem ends and cores, and quarter tomatoes. Use a small spoon to scrape out the excess seeds, if desired. In 4- to 6-quart kettle or Dutch oven combine all ingredients. Bring mixture to boiling; boil, uncovered, 5 minutes.

Ladle hot soup into hot jars, leaving ½-inch headspace. Adjust lids. Process in pressure canner at 10 pounds (pints) 45 minutes; (quarts) 55 minutes. Makes 8 pints.

MEAT, POULTRY, AND FISH

In days gone by, canning meat, fish, or poultry at home was left to the farmer's wife or daughter and the spouse of a hunter or fisherman. In some areas this is still true. But today in cities across the country, the homemaker who uses a pressure canner for vegetables can now include meats by taking advantage of the good buys on pot roasts, chickens, and fish at her nearby market. Canning these bargains not only stretches the budget, but also provides a shelfful of convenience foods, ready to serve after a short boil (tip box, page 44).

Getting Meat, Poultry, and Fish Ready

Beef, pork, lamb, veal, and large game: Chill home-dressed meat or large game immediately. Can the meat as soon as the carcass has reached a temperature of 40° or below. Refrigerate purchased meat and can as soon after purchase as possible. Cut the chilled meat into cubes or strips that will pack easily into canning jars. Make sure that the grain of the meat runs lengthwise. Trim away all of the visible fat and the connective tissue.

Ground meat: Grind only less-tender cuts of meat that are fresh, clean, chilled, and trimmed of fat and connective tissue for use in meatballs, chili, and other home-canned meat mixtures. Discard lumps of fat and never combine scraps of meat of differing freshness.

Poultry, game birds, and rabbit: Chill the meat immediately after cleaning and dressing. If poultry is purchased at a meat counter, be sure to keep it thoroughly chilled during the trip home. Then, can it immediately. Depending upon maturity, chicken and small game birds may be canned without boning. In general, process young birds after cutting them up.

Main dishes from the shelf

← *After a 10-minute simmering, spicy* Fish Creole *(page 44),* Garden Pea Soup *with ham (page 40), and hearty* Old-Fashioned Beef Stew *(page 40) are piping hot and ready to serve.*

Remove the breastbone and cut the drumsticks short enough to fit into the jar. Roast or simmer larger or more mature birds, and remove the bones before canning the meat.

Fish: Can only very fresh, thoroughly cleaned fish. Split the fish, but do not remove the backbone. Soak the fish 1 hour in a brine solution made in the proportion of 1 cup salt to 1 gallon of water. Follow recipe directions for kinds of sauces and seasonings to add.

Packing the Jars

After the meat or fish has been cleaned and handled or precooked as directed, you are ready to pack the jars. There is less shrinkage of precooked meats that are packed hot, but you may like the texture of the canned meats better if they are packed raw.

Complete step-by-step directions and photographs showing how to fill the jars begin on page 12. Be sure to leave 1-inch headspace at the top of jars of meat, poultry, and fish products. Fill with broth or seasoned sauce to within 1 inch of the top.

Pressure Processing

Process all home-canned foods containing meat in a pressure canner for a specified amount of time. You'll find these times in the charts and recipes. Many of the times will appear long, but they are necessary to destroy heat-resistant bacteria. Since the times are not related to the doneness of the meat, *do not shorten* processing times in hopes of getting a less well-done final product. Likewise, after opening the jars, boil all home-canned meats and meat products at least 10 minutes before tasting or serving them.

Look for detailed information on how to use a pressure canner on page 14. This information covers how to bring up the pressure of the canner and maintain it, as well as how to know when the pressure is down to normal. Also follow information in the tip box on page 15, if you need an altitude correction for the area of the country in which you live.

Canning Meat, Poultry, and Fish

Meat	Preparation of Meat	Pressure canner minutes at 10 lbs. (pints)	Pressure canner minutes at 10 lbs. (quarts)
Beef Lamb Pork Veal Venison	Chill meat immediately after slaughter. Wipe meat with clean, damp cloth. Cube meat or cut meat into jar-length pieces so grain runs length of jar. Remove gristle, bones, and as much fat as possible. *Raw Pack:* Pack loosely into hot jars, leaving 1-inch headspace. Add ½ teaspoon salt to each quart jar. Do not add liquid. Adjust lids. Process. *Hot Pack:* Simmer meat in a small amount of water in a covered pan till medium-done; stir occasionally. Season lightly with salt. *Or* brown the meat in small amount of fat. Season lightly with salt. Pack the meat loosely into hot jars, leaving 1-inch headspace. Fill with boiling water or broth, leaving 1-inch headspace. Adjust lids. Process.	75 75	90 90
Poultry Chicken	Rinse chilled, dressed chicken in cold water. Pat dry with clean cloth. Cut up chicken. Remove visible fat. *Raw Pack:* Do not remove bones (except breastbone, if desired). Pack the chicken pieces loosely into hot jars as follows: place thigh and drumsticks with skin next to glass and fit breast pieces into center, leaving 1-inch headspace. Add ½ teaspoon salt to each quart. Do not add liquid. Adjust lids. Process. *Hot Pack:* Boil, steam, or bake chicken just until meat can be removed from the bone. Take meat off bones, if desired, but do not remove skin. Pack chicken pieces loosely into hot jars as follows: place thigh and drumsticks with skin next to glass and fit breast pieces into the center, leaving 1-inch headspace. Add ½ teaspoon salt to each quart. Cover with boiling water or broth, leaving 1-inch headspace. Adjust lids. Process.	Bone-in 65 Boned 75 Bone-in 65	75 90 75
Duck Turkey Game birds	Rinse chilled, dressed poultry in cold water. Pat dry with a clean cloth. Pack small birds according to directions for chicken. Simmer or roast unstuffed larger birds just till meat can be removed from bone. *Hot Pack:* Cut precooked poultry into pieces of convenient size to pack in jars. Pack the meat loosely into hot jars, leaving 1-inch headspace. Add ½ teaspoon salt to each quart jar. Fill jars with boiling water or broth, leaving 1-inch headspace. Adjust lids. Process.	Boned 75 Bone-in 65	90 75
Rabbit	Rinse rabbit thoroughly in cold water; cut up. For wild rabbit soak meat 1 to 2 hours in salt water made from ¼ cup salt and 1 quart water. Rinse. Pat dry with clean cloth. Pack according to directions for chicken.	Boned 75 Bone-in 65	90 75

Fish	Preparation of Fish	Pressure canner minutes at 10 lbs. (pints)	Pressure canner minutes at 10 lbs. (quarts)
Bass Mackerel Salmon Trout	Rinse well-cleaned fish in fresh water. Split, but do not remove backbone. Remove skin, if desired. Make brine solution, using 1 cup salt and 1 gallon water. Soak the fish in brine for 30 to 60 minutes, depending upon the thickness of the fish. Drain and rinse fish; discard brine. *Raw Pack:* Cut fish into pieces about 1 inch shorter than jar length. Pack fish so that the skin side of the pieces is next to the glass. Alternate head and tail ends if small fish are being packed. Pack fish into hot jars, leaving 1-inch headspace. Do not add liquid or oil. Add ½ teaspoon salt to each quart jar. Adjust lids. Process.	100	100

Add robust flavor to Lemon Beef Steak *(page 49) by using your home-canned* Beef Soup Stock *(page 40). This full-bodied stock will fast become a favorite seasoning for recipes calling for beef stock.*

OLD-FASHIONED BEEF STEW

This hearty stew (shown on page 36) gets its full flavor from meat cubes browned before canning—

2½ pounds beef stew meat, cut in
      1-inch cubes
¼ cup shortening
2 cups water
5 cups carrots cut in ½-inch slices
5 cups cubed, peeled potatoes
1 cup chopped onion
1 cup chopped celery
2 cloves garlic, minced
1 tablespoon salt
2 teaspoons Worcestershire sauce
1 teaspoon paprika
⅛ teaspoon pepper
¼ cup all-purpose flour
½ cup cold water

In 4- to 6-quart kettle or Dutch oven brown half the meat at a time in hot shortening. In kettle combine browned meat, 2 cups water, carrots, potatoes, onion, celery, garlic, salt, Worcestershire sauce, paprika, and pepper; cook, covered, 15 minutes. Combine flour and ½ cup cold water; add to boiling stew mixture. Cook and stir till bubbly. (Mixture will appear thin before canning.)

Pack in hot jars, distributing meat, vegetables, and gravy evenly, and leaving 1-inch headspace. Adjust lids. Process in pressure canner at 10 pounds pressure (pints) 75 minutes; (quarts) 90 minutes. Makes 8 pints.

CHICKEN STOCK

6 to 7 pounds bony chicken pieces
      (backs, necks, and wings)
3 stalks celery with leaves, cut up
1 large onion, cut in wedges

Cover chicken with 2 quarts water. Add celery, onion, 2 teaspoons salt, and ¼ teaspoon pepper. Bring the mixture to boiling; reduce heat. Simmer, covered, for 1 hour. Remove large pieces of bones, chicken, and vegetables; strain remaining stock and skim off the fat.

Pour hot stock into hot jars, leaving 1-inch headspace. Adjust lids. Process in pressure canner at 10 pounds pressure (pints) 20 minutes; (quarts) 25 minutes. Makes 4 pints.

BEEF SOUP STOCK

4 pounds beef shanks and beef bones
3 carrots, cut in 1-inch pieces
3 stalks celery with leaves, cut up
1 large onion, cut in wedges
4 quarts water
¼ of small head cabbage
1 tablespoon salt
3 cloves garlic, halved
3 sprigs parsley
10 peppercorns
2 bay leaves

Have meatman break beef bones. Place beef shanks and bones, carrots, celery, and onion in roasting pan. Roast at 375° till meat has browned, 1 hour, stirring occasionally. Transfer mixture to 8- to 10-quart kettle or Dutch oven. Add remaining ingredients. Bring to boiling; cover and reduce heat. Simmer 3 hours.

Remove large pieces of bones, meat, and vegetables; strain remaining stock and skim off fat. Pour hot soup stock into hot jars, leaving 1-inch headspace. Adjust lids. Process in the pressure canner at 10 pounds pressure (pints) 20 minutes. Makes 6 pints.

GARDEN PEA SOUP

This soup is one of the trio shown on page 36—

5 cups shelled fresh green peas
1½ to 2 cups finely chopped ham
1 cup finely chopped onion
¾ cup chopped celery
1 teaspoon salt
½ teaspoon pepper
½ teaspoon dried marjoram, crushed

In 4- to 6-quart kettle or Dutch oven cover peas with boiling water; cook 12 to 15 minutes. Drain peas; press through food mill or blend smooth in blender. Return to kettle.

Add 3½ cups water, ham, onion, celery, and seasonings. Heat to boiling. Ladle hot soup into hot jars, leaving ½-inch headspace. Adjust lids. Process in pressure canner at 10 pounds pressure (pints) 60 minutes; (quarts) 75 minutes. Makes 4 pints.

Before serving: Boil, uncovered, at least 10 minutes *before* tasting or using. To serve, add ½ cup milk for each pint; heat through.

PEPPERPOT SOUP

        1 pound honeycomb tripe
        1 cup chopped green pepper
        ½ cup chopped onion
        ½ cup chopped celery
        2 tablespoons butter, melted
        2 tablespoons all-purpose flour
        6 chicken bouillon cubes
        1 teaspoon celery salt

Combine 4 cups boiling water and 1 teaspoon salt. Add tripe; simmer, covered, 2½ to 3 hours. Drain. Finely dice tripe. Combine next 4 ingredients. Blend in flour; add bouillon cubes and 6 cups boiling water. Cook and stir till bubbly. Add diced tripe, celery salt, and ¼ teaspoon pepper. Cover; bring to boiling.

Pack hot soup into hot jars, leaving 1-inch headspace. Adjust lids. Process in pressure canner at 10 pounds pressure (pints) 75 minutes; (quarts) 90 minutes. Makes 4 pints.

Before serving: Boil, uncovered, at least 10 minutes *before* tasting or using. Slowly add ¼ cup light cream for each pint; heat through.

CHICKEN NOODLE SOUP

        1 2½- to 3-pound ready-to-cook
            broiler-fryer chicken, cut up
        ½ teaspoon dried thyme, crushed
        ¼ teaspoon dried oregano, crushed
        1 cup diced celery
        ½ cup chopped onion
        ½ cup chopped carrots

Cover chicken with 3 quarts water. Add thyme and oregano. Bring to boiling; simmer, covered, 1 hour. Remove chicken from broth; cool. Remove meat from bones; dice. Strain broth; skim off fat. Return broth to kettle; add chicken, celery, onion, carrots, 1 tablespoon salt, and ¼ teaspoon pepper. Bring to boiling. Reduce heat and cook, covered, 10 minutes, stirring the mixture occasionally.

Pour hot soup into hot jars, leaving 1-inch headspace. Adjust lids. Process in pressure canner at 10 pounds pressure (pints) 75 minutes; (quarts) 90 minutes. Makes 5 pints.

Before serving: For each pint, add 1 cup water; boil, uncovered, at least 10 minutes *before* using. Add ½ cup cooked noodles; heat.

HAM-BEAN SOUP

        1 pound dry navy beans (2 cups)
        1 meaty ham bone
        ½ cup chopped onion
        6 whole black peppercorns
        1 bay leaf

Rinse beans; add to 2 quarts water. Bring to boiling; reduce heat and simmer 2 minutes. Remove from heat. Cover; let stand 1 hour. Add ham bone, onion, and 1 teaspoon salt. Tie peppercorns and bay leaf in cheesecloth; add to mixture. Simmer, covered, 1 hour. Remove spice bag and ham bone. Cut off meat and dice; measure 1½ cups. Add ham. Heat.

Pack hot soup into hot jars, leaving 1-inch headspace. Adjust lids. Process in pressure canner at 10 pounds pressure (pints) 75 minutes; (quarts) 90 minutes. Makes 4 pints.

Before serving: Add ¾ cup water to each pint of ham-bean soup. Boil, uncovered, at least 10 minutes *before* tasting or using.

FISH STEW

        2 pounds dressed fresh fish, boned and
            skinned
        6 large tomatoes, peeled, stem ends and
            cores removed, and cut up
        2 cloves garlic, finely chopped
        2 teaspoons sugar
        ½ teaspoon celery salt
            Dash cayenne
        4 cups peeled and cubed potatoes
        ½ cup chopped onion
        ¼ cup chopped canned pimiento
        3 slices bacon, crisp-cooked, drained,
            and crumbled
        1 tablespoon lemon juice

Cut fish into 1-inch pieces. Soak for 1 hour in brine solution made of 8 cups water and ½ cup salt. Drain fish. Combine 3 cups water, tomatoes, garlic, sugar, 1 teaspoon salt, celery salt, and cayenne. Cover and simmer 20 minutes. Add remaining ingredients. Bring to boiling; cook just to heat vegetables. Add fish. Pack into hot jars, leaving 1-inch headspace. Adjust lids. Process in pressure canner at 10 pounds pressure (pints and quarts) for 100 minutes. Makes 6 pints.

BASIC MEATBALLS

6 eggs
6 cups soft bread crumbs
1½ cups water
1 cup finely chopped onion
1 tablespoon salt
¼ teaspoon pepper
6 pounds ground beef

In large bowl combine first 6 ingredients. Add beef; mix well. Shape into 12 dozen 1-inch meatballs. Place in shallow baking pan. Bake at 425° for 15 minutes. Pack loosely into hot jars, leaving 1-inch headspace. Add boiling water or meat juice, leaving 1-inch headspace. Adjust lids. Process in pressure canner at 10 pounds pressure (pints) 75 minutes; (quarts) 90 minutes. Makes 8 pints.

CHILI CON CARNE

4 pounds ground beef
4 cups chopped onion
2 cups chopped green pepper
8 pounds tomatoes, peeled, stem ends
    and cores removed, and cut up
¼ cup sugar
2 tablespoons *each* salt and chili powder
1 teaspoon paprika
4 bay leaves, finely crushed

Brown the meat; drain off fat. Stir in remaining ingredients and 4 cups water. Bring to boiling. Reduce heat; simmer 30 minutes, stirring occasionally. Pack into hot jars, leaving 1-inch headspace. Adjust lids. Process in pressure canner at 10 pounds pressure (pints) 75 minutes; (quarts) 90 minutes. Makes 6 quarts.
   Before serving: Boil chili, uncovered, at least 10 minutes *before* tasting or using. Add 2 cups cooked and drained kidney beans to each quart of chili con carne. Heat through.

A fast entrée idea

← *Looking for a way to use canned* Mixed Vegetables *(page 33) and* Beef *(page 38)? Then try* Shortcut Shepherd's Pie *(page 48). Top each pie with a mound of instant potatoes and a cheese triangle.*

BASIC GROUND BEEF

4 pounds ground beef
2 cups chopped celery
2 cups chopped onion
1 cup chopped green pepper

In 4- to 6-quart kettle or Dutch oven cook meat, vegetables, and 2 teaspoons salt for 15 minutes. Drain off excess fat. Pack hot mixture into hot jars, leaving 1-inch headspace. Add boiling water or meat juice, leaving 1-inch headspace. Adjust lids. Process in pressure canner at 10 pounds pressure (pints) 75 minutes; (quarts) 90 minutes. Makes 6 pints.

ITALIAN MEAT SAUCE

12 pounds tomatoes
2 tablespoons sugar
1 tablespoon dried oregano, crushed
1 tablespoon dried thyme, crushed
2 bay leaves
1 pound ground beef
2 cups chopped onion
1 cup chopped green pepper
2 cloves garlic, crushed

Remove stem ends and cores and chop tomatoes; measure about 24 cups. Let chopped tomatoes stand in colander for a few minutes to drain off excess liquid. In 8- to 10-quart kettle or Dutch oven combine tomatoes, sugar, 1 tablespoon salt, oregano, thyme, ½ teaspoon pepper, and bay leaves. Boil gently, uncovered, for 1 hour. Strain through food mill; measure about 11 cups tomato purée. Return purée to kettle. Boil gently, uncovered, till of desired consistency, about 1 hour.
   Meanwhile, in skillet cook ground beef, onion, chopped green pepper, and garlic till meat is browned and onion and green pepper are tender; drain off fat. Add meat mixture to tomato purée in kettle and heat through.
   Pack hot meat sauce into hot jars, leaving 1-inch headspace. Adjust lids. Process in pressure canner at 10 pounds pressure (pints) 75 minutes; (quarts) 90 minutes. Makes 5 pints.
   Before serving: Boil meat sauce, uncovered, for at least 10 minutes *before* tasting or using. Serve Italian Meat Sauce over hot cooked spaghetti. Pass Parmesan cheese, if desired.

FISH CREOLE

This Southern favorite is pictured on page 36—

  3 pounds dressed fresh fish, boned and
    skinned
  1 cup chopped onion
  1 cup chopped celery
  2 cloves garlic, minced
  ¼ cup cooking oil
  6 tomatoes
  2 8-ounce cans tomato sauce
  2 tablespoons Worcestershire sauce
  2½ teaspoons salt
  2 teaspoons sugar
  ½ teaspoon chili powder
  ¼ teaspoon bottled hot pepper sauce
  4 teaspoons cornstarch
  1 cup chopped green pepper

Cut fish into 1-inch pieces. Soak for 1 hour in brine solution made of 8 cups water and ½ cup salt. Drain. Meanwhile, in 4- to 6-quart kettle or Dutch oven cook onion, celery, and garlic in cooking oil till tender but not brown.

Wash tomatoes; peel and remove stem ends and cores. Cut up tomatoes and add to onion mixture with tomato sauce, ½ cup water, Worcestershire, salt, sugar, chili powder, and hot pepper sauce. Bring to boiling. Mix cornstarch with 1 tablespoon cold water; stir into hot sauce. Cook and stir till bubbly. Add green pepper; heat mixture through.

Put ½ pound fresh fish into *each* hot pint jar or 1 pound fish into *each* hot quart jar. Pour hot tomato mixture over fish, leaving 1-inch headspace. Adjust lids. Process in pressure canner at 10 pounds pressure (pints or quarts) 100 minutes. Makes 6 pints.

Before serving: Boil, uncovered, at least 10 minutes *before* tasting or using. Serve Fish Creole over hot cooked rice.

Boiling home-canned meat

Before tasting or using home-canned meat, poultry, or fish, always boil it, uncovered, for at least 10 minutes. Add water as needed to prevent sticking. Do not taste these foods cold from the jar.

SWISS STEAK

  ½ cup all-purpose flour
  4 pounds beef round steak, cut 1 inch
    thick
  ¼ cup shortening
  3 cups cut-up, peeled tomatoes
  2 cups sliced fresh mushrooms
  1 cup chopped onion
  ½ cup chopped green pepper
  1 tablespoon sugar

Combine flour, 2 teaspoons salt, and ½ teaspoon pepper; pound into meat. Cut meat in serving-size pieces. Brown the meat in hot shortening; drain. Pack meat in hot jars, leaving 1-inch headspace. Combine remaining ingredients; bring sauce to boiling. Pour sauce over steak, leaving 1-inch headspace. Adjust lids. Process in pressure canner at 10 pounds pressure (quarts) 90 minutes. Makes 3 quarts.

Before serving: Boil, uncovered, at least 10 minutes *before* tasting or using. For each quart, combine ¼ cup cold water and 2 tablespoons all-purpose flour. Slowly add to meat mixture; cook and stir till thickened and bubbly.

CHICKEN À LA KING

In 8- to 10-quart kettle or Dutch oven place two 5-pound stewing chickens, cut in pieces. Cover chicken with water. Add 1 cup chopped celery; ½ cup chopped onion; and 1 clove garlic, minced. Bring mixture to boiling. Reduce heat and simmer, covered, till chicken is barely tender, about 2 hours. Cool.

Remove chicken pieces from broth. Remove skin and bones from chicken; cut meat into cubes. Remove excess chicken fat from broth; reserve 1 cup fat. Strain broth; reserve 8 cups.

Melt fat; blend in 1⅓ cups all-purpose flour and 4 teaspoons salt. Add reserved broth; cook and stir till bubbly. Add chicken, 2 cups sliced fresh mushrooms, 1 cup chopped canned pimiento, and ½ cup chopped green pepper. Simmer 5 minutes. Pack into hot jars, leaving 1-inch headspace. Adjust lids. Process in pressure canner at 10 pounds pressure (pints) 65 minutes. Makes 9 pints.

Before serving: Boil chicken, uncovered, at least 10 minutes *before* tasting or using. Add milk till of desired consistency.

BEEF STROGANOFF

3 pounds beef round steak, cut in
    1-inch cubes
¼ cup all-purpose flour
⅓ cup cooking oil
4 cups sliced fresh mushrooms
1½ cups chopped onion
3 cloves garlic, minced
6 tablespoons butter
½ cup all-purpose flour
¼ cup tomato paste
3 10½-ounce cans condensed beef broth

Coat steak with flour; brown the meat in oil. Remove from pan. Add mushrooms, onion, and garlic; cook 3 minutes. Remove vegetables; add butter to pan drippings. Blend in flour and tomato paste. Stir in broth. Cook and stir till bubbly. Add meat and vegetable mixture; heat. Pack into hot jars, leaving 1-inch headspace. Adjust lids. Process in pressure canner at 10 pounds pressure (pints) 75 minutes; (quarts) 90 minutes. Makes 4 to 5 pints.

Before serving: Boil, uncovered, at least 10 minutes *before* tasting or using. For each pint, add ½ cup dairy sour cream; heat through. Serve over hot buttered noodles.

CURRIED LAMB

4 pounds lean lamb, cut in 1-inch cubes
¼ cup shortening
2 cups chopped onion
2 cloves garlic, minced
4 tomatoes, peeled, stem ends and cores
    removed, and cut up
1 tablespoon curry powder
¼ cup all-purpose flour

Brown the meat in shortening; remove meat. Add onion and garlic; cook till tender but not brown. Return meat to skillet. Add tomatoes, curry, and 2 teaspoons salt; heat to boiling. Blend flour and ½ cup cold water; stir into meat mixture. Cook and stir till bubbly. Pack into hot jars, leaving 1-inch headspace. Adjust lids. Process in pressure canner at 10 pounds pressure (pints) 75 minutes. Makes 4½ pints.

Before serving: Boil, uncovered, at least 10 minutes *before* tasting or using. Serve with hot cooked rice.

BARBECUE SANDWICHES

2 29-ounce cans tomato sauce
2 cups chopped onion
½ cup chopped green pepper
¼ cup packed brown sugar
¼ cup Worcestershire sauce
2 tablespoons dry mustard
2 teaspoons salt
¼ teaspoon bottled hot pepper sauce
¼ cup mixed pickling spices
4 pounds cooked pork or beef,
    coarsely chopped (6 cups)

Combine first 8 ingredients. Tie pickling spices in cheesecloth bag; add to sauce. Cover and simmer 15 minutes. Remove spice bag and add meat to sauce. Cover; heat. Pack into hot jars, leaving 1-inch headspace. Adjust lids. Process in pressure canner at 10 pounds pressure (pints) 75 minutes. Makes 5 pints.

Before serving: Boil, uncovered, at least 10 minutes *before* tasting or using. Serve in buns.

HOMEMADE MINCEMEAT

1 pound beef stew meat
4 pounds apples, peeled, cored,
    and cut up
4 ounces suet
1 15-ounce package raisins (3¾ cups)
2½ cups sugar
2½ cups water
1 8-ounce package currants (2 cups)
½ cup diced candied fruits and peels
1 teaspoon grated orange peel
1 cup orange juice
1 teaspoon grated lemon peel
¼ cup lemon juice
1 teaspoon salt
½ teaspoon ground nutmeg
¼ teaspoon ground mace

Simmer beef, covered, in water till tender, about 2 hours. Cool. Put through coarse blade of food chopper with apples and suet. Combine with remaining ingredients in large kettle. Cover and simmer 1 hour; stir often.

Pack hot mincemeat into hot jars, leaving 1-inch headspace. Adjust lids. Process in pressure canner at 10 pounds pressure (pints and quarts) 20 minutes. Makes 6 pints.

EDITORS' CHOICE

Are you searching for different ways to take advantage of the goodness and versatility in your supply of home-canned products? If so, the recipes and menu suggestions on the following pages are just for you.

All of the recipes in this section are adaptations of popular dishes. Home-canned foods are listed in pint or quart measurements, and the directions reflect proper cooking techniques. A quick glance at the recipes will show you that the most important change is in those recipes using low-acid vegetables, meats, or fish. Remember that when preparing a recipe with these particular foods, you must boil them gently for at least 10 minutes *before* tasting or combining them with other ingredients. Be sure to keep this step in mind as you adapt your own favorite recipes, too.

The menus found on page 55 incorporate several home-canned products. They make use of jellies and pickles as well as fruits, vegetables, and meats. Each of the menus was planned around delicious flavor and good nutrition as well as eye appeal. You may not have canned the entire group of foods suggested, but there is enough variety to give you many helpful serving ideas.

Look on these home-canned products as convenience foods. After all, the time-consuming cleaning, cutting, and precooking were done at the time the foods were canned. Now you have the jars of prepared food at your fingertips. And, since all of these canned foods are shelf stable, they are ready to use without having to wait for the food to thaw.

Handy home-canned foods play several roles in family meal planning and preparation. They are tasty reminders of summer's abundance. For example, start any meal with a flavorful fruit or vegetable juice. Use chilled fruits as a refreshing dessert either by themselves or spooned over ice cream or plain cake. Likewise, tender meats and garden vegetables, after the necessary boiling, may be served without further attention. Finally, call upon jellies and pickles to add that special touch that makes a meal remarkable.

BEEF BURGUNDY

½ pint canned whole Mushrooms (page 31)
1½ pounds beef round steak, cut ¼ inch thick
2 tablespoons butter or margarine
½ cup coarsely chopped onion
2 teaspoons finely snipped parsley
1 small clove garlic, crushed
1 small bay leaf
½ teaspoon salt
Dash pepper
1 cup water
¾ cup Burgundy
1 tablespoon cornstarch
1 tablespoon cold water
Hot cooked rice *or* noodles

Place canned mushrooms and liquid in small saucepan; boil gently, uncovered, at least 10 minutes *before* tasting or using. Drain; set aside. Trim fat from round steak; cut meat into bite-size cubes. Melt butter or margarine in a medium skillet. Brown the steak pieces on all sides in the butter. Remove meat; keep warm. Add chopped onion to skillet; cook till tender but not brown. Add parsley, garlic, bay leaf, salt, and pepper.

Stir in the mushrooms, meat cubes, water, and Burgundy. Heat mixture to boiling. Reduce heat and simmer, covered, till meat is tender, about 1 hour. Remove bay leaf.

Blend cornstarch and cold water; stir slowly into hot mixture. Cook and stir till thickened and bubbly. If desired, transfer Beef Burgundy to blazer pan of chafing dish; place over water bath to keep warm. Serve over hot cooked rice or noodles. Makes 6 servings.

Perfect for a buffet

← *The next time you entertain extra-special guests, dazzle them by serving* Beef Burgundy. *Very few entrées match its elegance and eye appeal. This dish features home-canned* Mushrooms *(page 31).*

HAMBURGER-CHEESE BAKE

    1 pint canned Basic Ground Beef (page 43)
    2 8-ounce cans tomato sauce
    1 teaspoon sugar
    ¼ teaspoon garlic salt
    6 ounces uncooked medium noodles
    1 cup cream-style cottage cheese
    1 8-ounce package cream cheese, softened
    ¼ cup dairy sour cream
    ¼ cup grated Parmesan cheese (optional)

Boil meat, uncovered, at least 10 minutes *before* tasting or using. Stir in tomato sauce, sugar, garlic salt, and ¼ teaspoon pepper; remove from heat. Cook noodles; drain. Mix cottage cheese, cream cheese, and sour cream.

    Layer *half* noodles in 11x7½x1½-inch baking pan; add *half* hot meat sauce; cover with cheese mixture. Add rest of noodles and meat sauce; sprinkle with Parmesan cheese. Bake at 350° for 30 minutes. Serves 8 to 10.

CHICKEN CURRY

    2 quarts canned Chicken parts (page 38)
    2 tablespoons cooking oil
    ½ cup chopped onion
    1 clove garlic, minced
    1 tablespoon curry powder
    1 tablespoon cornstarch
    ½ teaspoon sugar
    1 medium tomato, peeled and chopped
    Curry condiments
    Saffron Rice

Boil chicken, uncovered, at least 10 minutes *before* tasting or using; drain, reserving 1½ cups broth. Bone chicken. Heat oil. Cook onion and garlic in oil till tender but not brown. Mix curry, cornstarch, and sugar; blend into mixture. Add tomato and reserved broth; cook and stir till thickened. Stir in chicken; heat.

    Serve with condiments such as chutney, kumquats, shredded coconut, and peanuts. Pass Saffron Rice. Makes 6 servings.

    Saffron Rice: In 1-quart casserole dissolve ½ teaspoon crushed threaded saffron in ¼ cup hot water. Add ¾ cup uncooked long grain rice, 2 tablespoons butter, and ¼ teaspoon salt. Stir in 1¼ cups boiling water. Bake, uncovered, at 450° for 25 to 30 minutes.

SHORTCUT SHEPHERD'S PIE

    1 pint canned Mixed Vegetables (page 33)
    1 tablespoon instant minced onion
    2 tablespoons butter or margarine
    2 tablespoons all-purpose flour
    1 14½-ounce can evaporated milk
    1 pint canned Beef (page 38)
    Packaged instant mashed potatoes
      (enough for 4 servings)
    2 slices process American cheese

Boil vegetables and instant onion, uncovered, at least 10 minutes *before* tasting or using; do not drain. Stir in butter. Blend flour and *1 cup* evaporated milk; stir into mixture. Cook and stir till thickened and bubbly.

    Boil beef, uncovered, at least 10 minutes *before* tasting or using. Add beef to vegetable mixture; heat through. Turn into 4 individual casseroles. Prepare instant potatoes, substituting remaining evaporated milk for milk called for on package directions. Pile atop meat mixture. Cut each cheese slice into 2 triangles. Place 1 on each casserole. Broil 4 inches from heat 3 to 4 minutes. Serves 4.

ORIENTAL BEEF STEW

    1½ pounds beef stew meat, cut in 1-inch
      cubes
    2 tablespoons cooking oil
    2 cups water
    ½ cup chopped onion
    1 small clove garlic, minced
    1 pint canned Tomatoes, cut up (page 26)
    ¼ cup soy sauce
    ¼ teaspoon ground ginger
    1 green pepper, cut in strips (1 cup)
    3 tablespoons cornstarch
    Hot cooked rice

In large saucepan brown the stew meat in hot oil. Add water, onion, and garlic; bring to boiling. Reduce heat and simmer, covered, for 1 to 1¼ hours, stirring occasionally to keep from sticking. Stir in tomatoes, soy, and ginger. Cover and cook 20 to 30 minutes. Skim excess fat. Add green pepper. Blend cornstarch and 3 tablespoons cold water; stir into hot stew. Cook and stir till bubbly. Cook and stir 3 minutes. Serve with rice. Serves 4.

DILLED SALMON PIE

1 pint canned Salmon (page 39)
2 cups soft bread crumbs (2½ slices)
½ cup milk
1 slightly beaten egg
1 tablespoon chopped onion
1 tablespoon butter or margarine,
   melted
½ teaspoon salt
   Packaged instant mashed potatoes
     (enough for 4 servings)
1 egg
   Dill Sauce

Boil salmon, uncovered, at least 10 minutes *before* tasting or using; drain and finely flake salmon. Combine bread crumbs, milk, 1 egg, onion, melted butter, and salt till crumbs are moistened. Add salmon and mix thoroughly. Turn into greased 8-inch pie plate. Prepare instant potatoes according to package directions, *omitting the milk*. Beat in the remaining egg. Spoon potato mixture around edge of pie. Bake at 350° for 30 to 35 minutes. Serve wedges with warm Dill Sauce. Serves 4 to 6.

Dill Sauce: In saucepan melt 1 tablespoon butter or margarine. Blend in 1 tablespoon all-purpose flour. Add 1¼ cups milk, 1 teaspoon sugar, ¾ teaspoon dried dillweed, and ½ teaspoon salt. Cook and stir till thickened and bubbly. Combine ½ cup dairy sour cream and 1 tablespoon lemon juice. Gradually stir into hot mixture. Makes 1⅔ cups sauce.

BEEFED-UP BEANS

1 pint canned Basic Ground Beef (page 43)
1 28-ounce can pork and beans in
   tomato sauce (3½ cups)
½ cup catsup
1 tablespoon prepared mustard
1 teaspoon soy sauce
1 teaspoon Worcestershire sauce
   Crackers

Boil meat, uncovered, at least 10 minutes *before* tasting or using. Add beans, ½ cup water, catsup, prepared mustard, soy sauce, and Worcestershire sauce. Simmer, uncovered, for 20 minutes, stirring occasionally. Serve in bowls with crackers. Makes 4 or 5 servings.

LEMON BEEF STEAK

1 pint canned Beef Soup Stock (page 40)
1 pound beef sirloin steak
1 clove garlic, halved
3 tablespoons butter or margarine
   Salt
   Paprika
1 medium onion, sliced
1 lemon, thinly sliced
2 medium tomatoes, peeled and
   cut in wedges
2 tablespoons cornstarch
   Salt
   Hot cooked noodles

Boil canned beef stock, uncovered, at least 10 minutes *before* tasting or using; set aside. Rub meat with cut edge of garlic. Cut meat into 2x½-inch strips. Melt butter; add meat and brown quickly. Remove from heat; season meat with salt and paprika. Arrange onion and lemon slices over meat. Add ¾ *cup* of the stock; cover and simmer 20 to 25 minutes.

Add tomato wedges; cover and simmer till tomatoes are hot, about 2 minutes. Remove meat and vegetables; keep warm. Discard lemon slices. Combine cornstarch and remaining cooled beef stock; stir into pan juices. Cook and stir till mixture thickens and bubbles. Season with salt. Spoon meat mixture atop noodles on serving platter. Top with hot gravy. Pass parsley, if desired. Serves 4.

KRAUT RELISH STACK-UPS

This hearty sandwich is pictured on page 33 —

In saucepan heat ½ cup sugar and ½ cup vinegar till sugar is dissolved; cool. Combine 1 pint canned Sauerkraut, drained (page 32); ½ cup diced celery; ½ cup diced green pepper; ¼ cup diced onion; and one 2-ounce jar pimientos, drained and chopped (about ¼ cup). Combine vegetables with vinegar mixture. Chill. Makes 3 cups relish.

For each stack-up sandwich, spread a slice of dark rye bread with a little butter. Stack slices of ham and natural Swiss cheese atop bread. Add about ¼ cup drained relish. Then add a slice of salami and top sandwich with another slice of buttered rye bread. (Refrigerate remaining relish until needed.)

CREAM OF ASPARAGUS SOUP

    1 pint canned Asparagus pieces (page 30)
    ½ cup water
    1 cup light cream
    2 tablespoons butter, melted
    1 tablespoon all-purpose flour
    ¼ teaspoon salt
       Dash pepper

In medium saucepan combine undrained canned asparagus pieces and water. Boil asparagus, uncovered, at least 10 minutes *before* tasting or using. Blend light cream, melted butter, flour, salt, and pepper. Stir mixture into the heated asparagus pieces. Cook and stir till soup is hot. Makes 4 servings.

COMPANY CARROTS

    1 quart canned sliced Carrots (page 30)
    1 cup dairy sour cream
    1 3-ounce package cream cheese,
       softened
    3 tablespoons finely chopped green pepper
    2 tablespoons sliced green onion
    ½ teaspoon salt
    ½ teaspoon grated lemon peel

Boil carrots, uncovered, at least 10 minutes *before* tasting or using. Drain well. In medium saucepan combine sour cream, cream cheese, green pepper, sliced green onion, salt, and lemon peel. Stir in drained carrots; heat through, but do not boil. Makes 8 servings.

ORANGE-GLAZED BEETS

    1 pint canned whole small Beets (page 30)
    3 tablespoons butter or margarine
    ¼ cup Orange Marmalade (page 65)
    1 tablespoon orange juice

Boil beets, uncovered, at least 10 minutes *before* tasting or using; drain. Melt butter or margarine in medium skillet; stir in orange marmalade and orange juice. Add the drained beets. Cook and stir mixture over low heat till beets are heated through and glazed, 6 to 8 minutes. Garnish beets with thin slices of orange, if desired. Makes 4 servings.

SWISS CORN BAKE

This creamy corn dish (pictured on page 28) is bound to become a vegetable favorite —

    1 pint canned Whole Kernel
       Corn (page 31)
    1 6-ounce can evaporated milk (⅔ cup)
    2 beaten eggs
    2 tablespoons finely chopped onion
       Dash pepper
    1 cup shredded process Swiss cheese
       (4 ounces)
    1 cup soft bread crumbs
    2 tablespoons butter, melted

Boil corn, uncovered 20 minutes *before* tasting or using. Drain well. Combine corn, evaporated milk, eggs, chopped onion, pepper, and ¾ *cup* of the shredded cheese.

Turn mixture into a 10x6x1½-inch baking dish or a 1-quart casserole. Toss bread crumbs with the melted butter and the remaining ¼ cup shredded Swiss cheese. Sprinkle over corn mixture. Bake at 350° for 25 to 30 minutes. Garnish with green pepper rings, if desired. Makes 4 to 6 servings.

GREEN BEANS FAR EAST

Roll a strip of perky red pimiento into a rose for a gala garnish —

    1 quart canned Green Beans (page 30)
    1 5-ounce can water chestnuts,
       drained and sliced (⅔ cup)
    ½ cup finely chopped onion
    2 tablespoons butter or margarine
    1 cup dairy sour cream
    1 teaspoon sugar
    1 teaspoon seasoned salt
    1 teaspoon vinegar
       Dash pepper

Boil beans, uncovered, at least 10 minutes *before* tasting or using. Add water chestnuts; heat through. Meanwhile, cook onion in butter or margarine till tender but not brown. Stir in sour cream, sugar, seasoned salt, vinegar, and pepper. Heat mixture through, but do not boil. Drain the green beans; turn into a serving bowl. Top the beans with the sour cream mixture. Garnish with a pimiento rose, if desired. Makes 6 to 8 servings.

Omelet Elegante *is the ultimate for lunch or brunch. This fluffy egg omelet holds a buttery mixture of artichokes and home-canned* Mushrooms *(page 31). Hollandaise sauce adds the crowning touch.*

OMELET ELEGANTE

- ½ **pint canned sliced Mushrooms (page 31)**
- 2 **tablespoons butter or margarine**
- 1 **7-ounce can artichoke hearts,**
  - **drained and coarsely chopped**
  - **Dash pepper**
- 4 **egg whites**
- 2 **tablespoons water**
- ¼ **teaspoon salt**
- 4 **egg yolks**
- 1 **tablespoon butter or margarine**
  - **Blender Hollandaise Sauce**

Boil mushrooms, uncovered, at least 10 minutes *before* tasting or using; drain. Melt the 2 tablespoons butter. Add mushrooms, artichokes, and pepper. Cook and stir till hot; remove from heat and keep warm. Beat egg whites till frothy; add water and salt. Beat till stiff but not dry peaks form. Beat yolks till very thick and lemon-colored. Fold into whites.

Heat the 1 tablespoon butter or margarine in a 10-inch oven-going skillet till a drop of water sizzles. Pour the egg mixture into the hot skillet and spread mixture evenly with spatula, leaving omelet higher at sides. Reduce heat. Cook omelet slowly till puffed and set, 8 to 10 minutes. (Lift edge of omelet with spatula; bottom will be golden.) Place lightly browned omelet in 325° oven.

Bake omelet till knife inserted in center comes out clean, about 10 minutes. Loosen sides of omelet with spatula. Place artichoke mixture on half the omelet. Fold over and turn out onto warm platter. Serve with Blender Hollandaise Sauce. Serves 3 or 4.

Blender Hollandaise Sauce: Place 3 egg yolks, 4 teaspoons lemon juice, and a dash cayenne in blender container. Cover and quickly turn blender on and off. Heat ½ cup butter till melted and almost boiling. Turn blender on high speed; slowly pour in butter, blending till thick and fluffy, about 30 seconds.

CHERRY PUFF

1 pint canned tart red Cherries
   (page 20)
½ cup sugar
1 tablespoon quick-cooking tapioca
1 tablespoon butter or margarine
   Few drops red food coloring
2 egg whites
¼ teaspoon cream of tartar
⅓ cup sugar
2 egg yolks
½ teaspoon vanilla
⅓ cup sifted cake flour
   Vanilla ice cream

Drain cherries, reserving ¾ cup liquid. If necessary, add water to syrup to make ¾ cup. Chop cherries; add the reserved liquid, ½ cup sugar, and tapioca. Cook and stir till thickened and bubbly. Remove from heat; stir in butter and food coloring.

Beat egg whites, cream of tartar, and dash salt to soft peaks. Gradually add ⅓ cup sugar, beating till stiff peaks form. Beat egg yolks and vanilla till thick and lemon-colored. Fold yolks into whites. Sift flour over; fold into mixture. Pour cherry mixture into 8x8x2-inch baking dish. Carefully pour batter evenly over cherries. Bake at 325° for 30 minutes. Serve warm with ice cream. Serves 6.

APPLESAUCE HARVEST BREAD

½ cup butter or margarine
⅔ cup sugar
2 eggs
2 cups all-purpose flour
1 teaspoon baking soda
1 cup canned Applesauce (page 20)
¾ cup shredded natural Cheddar cheese
   (3 ounces)
½ cup chopped walnuts

Cream together butter and sugar till light and fluffy. Add eggs; beat well. Stir together thoroughly the flour, soda, and ½ teaspoon salt; add to creamed mixture. Stir in the applesauce, cheese, and nuts. Turn into a greased 9x5x3-inch loaf pan. Bake at 350° for 50 to 55 minutes. Cool 10 minutes in pan. Remove bread from pan; cool on rack. Makes 1 loaf.

APRICOT UPSIDE-DOWN CAKE

1 pint canned Apricot halves (page 20)
½ cup packed brown sugar
¼ cup butter or margarine, melted
½ cup shredded coconut
½ cup granulated sugar
⅓ cup shortening
1 egg
1 teaspoon vanilla
1 cup all-purpose flour
1½ teaspoons baking powder
¼ teaspoon salt

Drain the canned apricots, reserving the syrup. Combine the brown sugar, butter, and *2 tablespoons* of the reserved apricot syrup. Spoon syrup mixture into an 8x8x2-inch baking pan, and sprinkle with coconut. Add water to remaining syrup to make ½ cup.

Arrange apricots, cut side up, atop coconut in pan. Cream together granulated sugar and shortening till light. Add egg and vanilla; beat till fluffy. Stir together thoroughly the flour, baking powder, and salt; add alternately with ½ cup reserved syrup, beating after each addition. Spread over apricots. Bake at 350° for 40 minutes. Cool 5 minutes; invert on plate. Serve warm. Makes 6 servings.

SPICY PEAR COMPOTE

1 cup canned Whole Cranberry Sauce
   (page 23)
3 tablespoons sugar
1½ teaspoons lemon juice
⅛ teaspoon ground cinnamon
⅛ teaspoon ground ginger
1 pint canned Pear halves (page 21)
2 medium oranges, peeled, sliced,
   and halved

In a medium saucepan combine canned cranberry sauce, sugar, lemon juice, cinnamon, and ginger; bring mixture to boiling. Drain canned pears, reserving ¼ cup syrup. Cut pears in half lengthwise. Add pear quarters, orange slices, and the reserved pear syrup to cranberry mixture in saucepan; stir gently. Return to boiling. Reduce heat; cover and simmer 5 minutes. Cool slightly. Spoon fruit into serving dishes. Serves 6.

SPICED PEACH SALAD

Home-canned spiced peaches make this salad special enough for your favorite guests —

  2 3-ounce packages lemon-flavored
    gelatin
  2 cups boiling water
  2 pints canned Spiced Peaches (page 25)
  1 4-ounce container whipped cream
    cheese
  ¼ cup finely chopped celery
  2 tablespoons finely chopped walnuts

Dissolve the lemon-flavored gelatin in the boiling water. Drain the canned spiced peaches, reserving the syrup. Add enough additional water to the reserved syrup to make 2 cups liquid. Add the reserved syrup to the dissolved gelatin. Chill till partially set.

Pour 1½ cups of the lemon-flavored gelatin mixture into a 10x6x2-inch baking dish. Combine the whipped cream cheese, chopped celery, and chopped walnuts. Fill spiced peach cavities with cream cheese mixture.

Arrange the filled peach halves on the almost-set gelatin mixture. Gently spoon the remaining gelatin over and around the filled peach halves. Chill the salad till firm, several hours or overnight. Makes 8 servings.

FRUIT SALAD SQUARES

  1 3¾-ounce package strawberry soft-
    style whipped dessert mix
  1 pint canned Rosy Fruit Cocktail,
    drained (page 24)
  ¼ cup chopped walnuts
  ¼ cup mayonnaise or salad dressing
  ½ cup whipping cream
    Lettuce

Prepare dessert mix according to package directions. Chill prepared mixture 15 to 20 minutes. Fold in drained fruit cocktail, walnuts, and mayonnaise. Whip cream; fold into fruit mixture. Turn salad into a foil-lined 9x9x2-inch baking pan. Freeze till firm.

Let frozen salad stand at room temperature 10 to 15 minutes before serving. To serve, cut into squares and place on lettuce-lined plates. Top each serving with additional chopped walnuts, if desired. Makes 9 servings.

PEACH-CHERRY SALAD RING

  1 pint canned Dark Sweet Cherries
    (page 20)
  ½ cup sugar
  2 envelopes unflavored gelatin
  ½ teaspoon salt
  ½ cup lemon juice
  2 7-ounce bottles ginger ale
    (about 2 cups)
  1 pint canned Peaches, drained and
    diced (page 21)

Drain dark sweet cherries, reserving the syrup; add enough water to syrup to make 1¼ cups. Combine sugar, unflavored gelatin, and salt in saucepan; stir in reserved cherry syrup. Stir over medium heat till gelatin dissolves. Remove from heat; stir in lemon juice. Allow mixture to cool but not set.

Resting bottle on rim of pan, gradually pour in the ginger ale, stirring gently with up-and-down motion. Chill the mixture till partially set. Fold in cherries and diced peaches. Turn into 6½-cup ring mold. Chill mixture till firm, 4 to 6 hours or overnight. Unmold and garnish with greens and additional canned fruit, if desired. Serves 8 to 10.

Fruit Salad Squares *start with whipped dessert mix. You add mayonnaise,* Rosy Fruit Cocktail *(page 24), and walnuts, then fold in whipped cream.*

BLUEBERRY BUCKLE

  ½ cup butter or margarine
  1 cup sugar
  2 eggs
  1 teaspoon vanilla
  1 teaspoon grated lemon peel
  2 cups all-purpose flour
 2½ teaspoons baking powder
  ¼ teaspoon salt
  ½ cup milk
  1 pint canned Blueberries, drained
    (page 20)
  ½ cup sugar
  ½ cup all-purpose flour
  ½ teaspoon ground cinnamon
  ¼ cup butter or margarine

Cream ½ cup butter or margarine and 1 cup sugar. Add the eggs, vanilla, and lemon peel; beat till light and fluffy. Stir together thoroughly the 2 cups flour, baking powder, and salt. Add to creamed mixture alternately with the milk. Spread the mixture in a greased 11x7x1½-inch baking pan. Arrange the drained blueberries evenly over batter.

Mix ½ cup sugar, ½ cup flour, and cinnamon; cut in ¼ cup butter till crumbly. Sprinkle mixture over the blueberries. Bake at 350° till done, about 40 minutes. Cut in squares and serve warm. Makes 6 to 8 servings.

PEACH PIE

  1 quart canned Peach halves (page 21)
  2 tablespoons cornstarch
  ¼ teaspoon ground mace
  ½ cup red currant jelly
  1 baked 9-inch pastry shell, cooled
    Whipped cream (optional)

Drain peaches, reserving ⅔ cup syrup. Slice peach halves. Combine cornstarch and mace in a small saucepan. Stir in the reserved peach syrup and the red currant jelly. Cook and stir till thickened and bubbly, about 5 minutes. Cool the mixture slightly.

Arrange the peaches in a single layer in the cooled, baked pastry shell, forming circles, one inside the other. Spoon the cooled glaze over the peaches. Chill thoroughly. Trim with whipped cream, if desired.

PEACH SHORTCAKE

  2 cups all-purpose flour
  2 tablespoons sugar
  3 teaspoons baking powder
  ½ teaspoon salt
  ½ cup butter or margarine
  1 beaten egg
 ⅔ cup milk
  1 quart canned Peach halves (page 21)
  2 tablespoons cornstarch
  2 tablespoons butter or margarine
  1 teaspoon lemon juice
    Dash ground nutmeg
    Whipped cream (optional)

Sift together thoroughly the first 4 ingredients. Cut in ½ cup butter till mixture resembles coarse crumbs. Combine egg and milk; add all at once, stirring just to moisten. Spread in greased 8x1½-inch round baking pan, building up edges slightly. Bake at 450° for 15 to 18 minutes. Remove from pan; cool 5 minutes.

Split cake in 2 layers. Drain peaches, reserving 1½ cups syrup. Slice peaches. Gradually stir reserved syrup into cornstarch. Cook and stir till thickened. Remove from heat; stir in 2 tablespoons butter, lemon juice, and nutmeg. Stir in peaches. Spread bottom cake layer with *half* of the peach mixture. Top with remaining cake and peaches. Pass whipped cream, if desired. Serves 6 to 8.

PEACH CRISP

  1 quart canned Peach halves (page 21)
    Few drops almond extract
 ⅔ cup packed brown sugar
  ½ cup all-purpose flour
  ½ cup quick-cooking rolled oats
  ¼ cup chopped pecans
  ¼ teaspoon ground nutmeg
  2 tablespoons butter or margarine
    Vanilla ice cream

Drain peaches, reserving ¼ cup syrup. Slice peaches. Arrange slices in 8x8x2-inch baking dish. Add almond extract to reserved syrup; pour over peaches. Combine next 5 ingredients; cut in butter till crumbly. Press mixture over peaches. Bake at 350° for 45 to 50 minutes. Serve warm with ice cream. Serves 6.

Menus Featuring Home-Canned Food

Looking for interesting meals that offer good eating? Nothing could be easier than one of these menus built around your supply of tasty home-canned foods. Here you will find favorite recipes interestingly combined to create delicious meals for your family or guests.

BREAKFAST

Apple-Cherry Juice*
Crisp Bacon
Waffles   Freezer Pineapple Conserve*
or
French Toast   Strawberry Syrup*
Coffee   Milk

SUNDAY BRUNCH

Pineapple-Grapefruit Juice*
Baked Eggs   Sausage Links
English Muffins   Sweet Cherry Jam*
or
Blueberry Buckle*
Milk   Coffee

LUNCH

Tomato Juice Cocktail*
Omelet Elegante*
Relish Tray
Peach Halves*
Milk   Tea

LUNCH

Barbecue Sandwiches*
Sweet Pickled Carrots*
Corn Chips or Potato Chips
Applesauce* à la Mode
Milk   Coffee

*See Index listing for page numbers

SUPPER

Old-Fashioned Beef Stew*
Kosher Dill Pickles*   Celery Sticks
Corn Bread Sticks   Butter
Lime Sherbet
Milk   Coffee

SUPPER

Hamburger-Cheese Bake*
Tossed Green Salad
Whole Wheat Rolls   Butter
Cherry Puff*
Tea   Milk

DINNER

Beef Stroganoff*   Noodles
Buttered Green Beans*
Peach-Cherry Salad Ring*
Watermelon Pickles*   Olives
Lemon Meringue Pie
Tea   Milk

DINNER

Grilled Pork Chops
Peas and Onions*
Spiced Peach Salad*
Dinner Rolls   Butter
Baked Apples
Coffee   Milk

Sharing homemade jellies and pickles with family and friends is part of the fun of making them. Pamper your family by having an assortment of colorful jams and tart, crisp pickles available for everyday meals. Then, draw on your supply of these handy items when setting the table for company—they add a personal dimension to a festive occasion. Or, tie ribbon around a jar and let it say welcome to a new neighbor or thank-you to a special friend. Your thoughtfulness will be appreciated everytime the gift is served.

How to Make
Jellies, Jams, and Pickles

Jellies, pickles, and all of their variations are not difficult to can. Follow the easy directions in this chapter to take the guesswork out of making jelly gel and to put the right spiciness in pickle products.

Start your jelly-making by using fresh fruits, or learn how to use canned or frozen juices in delicious fruit spreads. Make jams from crushed fruit, and enjoy the special flavor that lemon or orange peel give to marmalades and conserves.

Pickle carrots, beets, and onions individually, or choose a recipe that combines garden vegetables in an appetizing relish with peppy seasoning and crisp texture.

Center front: Orange Marmalade *(page 66), Clock-* →
wise: Watermelon Pickles *(page 76),* Sweet-Sour Pickles *(page 77),* Cherry-Peach Jam *(page 68), and* Pickled Mushrooms and Onions *(page 74).*

JELLIES AND JAMS

What is your favorite fruit spread—a shimmery jelly, a fruit-filled spreadable jam, or one of the variations such as a preserve, marmalade, or conserve?

Whatever your preference, the ingredients and the cooking techniques are similar. This has led to an understandable confusion in product names. Listed below are the definitions for the chief categories.

Jelly is made from fruit juice without any pieces of fruit. It is clear, shimmering, and quite firm, yet tender.

Jam is made from crushed or ground whole fruit rather than strained fruit juice. Although still firm enough to hold its shape, jam is usually softer than jelly.

Preserves consist of a thick syrup containing whole fruits or large fruit pieces.

Marmalade is jelly with pieces of fruit suspended in it. Citrus fruits including peel are frequently used for marmalade.

Conserve is a jamlike product made from a mixture of several fruits. At least one citrus fruit is usually included. A true conserve contains nuts and raisins.

Jelly Basics

To make jellies, jams, and the related products, use the open-kettle method of canning. In brief, cook the fruit mixture, uncovered, in a large kettle (see tip box) until it is ready to set up or gel. Ladle the hot mixture into hot, sterilized containers and seal. No further processing is needed because the high concentration of sugar acts as a preservative. Detailed instructions for cooking jellies and jams begin on page 60. Directions for uncooked, freezer jams are on page 62.

Day brighteners from the jam jar

← *Perk up breakfast by bringing out your homemade Apricot Jam or Red Plum Jam (recipes on page 67). These luscious fruit spreads add color and flavor interest to the morning muffins, toast, or rolls.*

Cook jelly in large kettle

Use an 8- to 10-quart kettle or Dutch oven for cooking jellies or jams. The pan looks large in proportion to the liquid, but the space is needed so the jelly or jam mixture can boil up the sides of the kettle without boiling over.

Many sizes and shapes of small glasses and jars are suitable for jellies and jams. Limit your choice to jars that can stand both the boiling needed to sterilize them and the temperature of the hot fruit mixture. For this reason, the best choices are standard half-pint jars or jelly glasses produced by canning jar manufacturers.

Several ingredients are common to jellies and similar products. These are fruit, pectin, sugar, and usually an acid. Each of these ingredients contributes to the finished product; without the proper balance, it is difficult to obtain a successful product.

Fruit provides the sought-after flavor in jellies and jam. While most homemakers make jelly when the fresh fruit is in season, you can make delicious jellies from canned or frozen fruit juices any time of year.

Pectin is the substance responsible for making jelly gel. It is naturally present in fruits, but the amounts vary. Apples, blackberries, cranberries, currants, gooseberries, slipskin grapes, sour plums, and citrus fruits contain considerable pectin. Slightly underripe fruit contains more pectin than does completely ripe fruit. Commercial fruit pectins are in two forms—liquid and powdered.

Strawberries, blueberries, peaches, apricots, rhubarb, pineapple, and cherries are low in pectin. Before the development of commercial pectin, you could not get these fruits to gel unless you combined them with fresh tart apple juice. Today, almost any fruit can be made to gel with commercial pectin.

Sugar is important in jelly–making for three reasons — it acts as a preservative, it develops the flavor by adding sweetness, and it aids in the formation of the gel.

Acid in the fruit works with the pectin in setting up the gel. It also contributes to the flavor of the jelly. Whenever fruit is low in acid, add lemon juice.

Making Jellies

1. Prepare the fruit juice. Soft fruits and juicy berries give up their juice readily when crushed. Firmer fruits must be softened by cooking before straining the juice. To do this, cut up the fruit but do not remove peel or core, as they contain the greatest concentration of pectin. Add just enough water to prevent fruit from sticking as it cooks. Excess water dilutes both the fruit flavor and the pectin (photo A).

Have a large square of clean muslin or several layers of cheesecloth ready to use as a jelly bag. Lay cloth loosely over a colander in a bowl. Prepare fruit and crush or strain it through the cloth (photo B). Tie corners of the cloth over the fruit so you can lift the bag and allow the juice to drip. Avoid squeezing the bag or you will get pulp along with juice and have a cloudy jelly.

2. Assemble jars and paraffin or flat metal lids and screw bands. Sterilize jars and let them stand in the hot water till needed. Melt paraffin, if used, in top of double boiler over hot water. Or, prepare flat metal lids according to manufacturer's directions.

3. Measure the fruit juice according to the recipe proportions into 8- to 10-quart kettle or Dutch oven. Do not double the jelly recipe. Instead, make two separate batches of jelly when you have a large quantity of juice. Four to six cups is about the right amount of juice for each batch of jelly.

4. Combine remaining ingredients and cook as indicated in recipe. The method of preparation is based on whether or not you add a commercial pectin. Jelly recipes begin on page 64.

With added pectin: Follow the recipe directions for combining fruit juice, pectin, and sugar. Powdered and liquid pectin are not interchangeable. Use the type specified.

Without added pectin: (Use only fruits that are high in natural pectin.) Cook the jelly at a

Wash, cut up, and put apples into a large kettle. Do not peel, core, or remove the seeds. Simmer in a minimum amount of water until tender.

Place layers of cheesecloth in a colander set in a bowl. Pour fruit and liquid into cloth and let juice drip through. Tie corners together for easy lifting.

To test for the jellying stage of jelly made without added pectin, dip a metal spoon in jelly. Watch for two drops that run together and sheet off the spoon.

full rolling boil until it reaches the jellying stage. The amount of time needed will vary from batch to batch and recipe to recipe, but there are two ways to tell when the jelly is ready. One is the sheeting-off test and the other is using a thermometer.

For the sheeting-off test, dip a cool metal spoon into the hot, bubbling jelly. Then, lift spoon about one foot above pan and let the jelly flow back into the kettle. When jelly has reached jellying stage, it will divide into two distinct drops that run together and sheet off the edge of the spoon (photo C).

If you're using a thermometer, first place it in boiling water to determine the exact temperature at which water boils in your area. Cook your jelly 8° beyond this boiling water temperature. For example, at sea level the jellying stage is 220° (212° plus 8°).

5. Remove pan from heat. Quickly skim off foam with metal spoon.

6. Pour or ladle hot jelly into sterilized hot jelly glasses or jars, and seal with paraffin or metal lids and screw bands. Follow directions and photographs that begin on page 62.

Making Jams, Marmalades, Conserves, and Preserves

1. Assemble jars and paraffin or flat metal lids and screw bands. Sterilize jars by boiling them in water for 10 minutes; let stand in water till needed. Melt paraffin in top of double boiler over hot water. Or, prepare flat metal lids according to manufacturer's directions.

2. Prepare fruit according to recipe.

3. Combine remaining ingredients and cook as indicated in the recipe. The method of preparation is based on whether or not you add a commercial pectin.

With added pectin: Follow the recipe directions. Procedures vary slightly for making jams, marmalades, conserves, and preserves. Powdered and liquid pectin are not interchangeable. Use the type specified.

Without added pectin: Cook all ingredients at full rolling boil till the desired thickness.

4. Remove pan from the heat. Stir and quickly skim off foam with a metal spoon.

5. Pour or ladle hot jam into hot sterilized jelly glasses or jars. Seal with paraffin or metal lids and screw bands. Directions for sealing cooked jellies and jams begin on page 62.

If your jelly doesn't gel

When jelly fails to gel, it is either because there was not enough pectin present, or because inaccurate measuring, insufficient cooking, overcooking, or a doubled recipe prevented the pectin from doing its job properly. Re-cooking may remedy the situation. If it doesn't, use the jelly as pancake or waffle syrup or spoon over ice cream.

If you used powdered or liquid pectin in the original jelly, add more of the same kind and follow the proportions and instructions given below.

If you did not add commercial pectin the first time, consider doing so. However, if you are certain the fruit juice was from high pectin-containing fruits that were not overripe, repeat the cooking process. Boil the jelly until the mixture reaches the jellying stage. Use either the sheeting-off test or a thermometer as a guide.

To recook jelly with powdered pectin: Measure the jelly to be recooked. For each quart of jelly, measure and set aside ¼ cup sugar, ¼ cup water, and 4 teaspoons powdered pectin. In saucepan or kettle mix the powdered pectin and water; bring to boiling, stirring constantly. Add the soft jelly and the sugar; stir thoroughly. Bring mixture to full rolling boil over high heat, stirring constantly. Boil hard for 30 seconds. Remove recooked jelly from heat; skim foam from top. Pour jelly into hot sterilized jars or jelly glasses; seal immediately.

To recook with liquid pectin: Measure the jelly to be recooked. For each quart of jelly, measure and set aside ¾ cup sugar, 2 tablespoons lemon juice, and 2 tablespoons liquid pectin. Bring jelly to boiling over high heat. Quickly add the sugar, lemon juice, and pectin, and bring to a full rolling boil, stirring constantly. Boil hard for 1 minute. Remove the recooked jelly from heat; skim off foam. Pour into hot sterilized containers and seal immediately.

Making Freezer Jellies, Jams, and Conserves

In this special group of spreads, the fruit and sugar are not cooked, thus providing fresh fruit flavor and easy preparation. The products are not shelf stable and must be either frozen or refrigerated and used within three weeks. To prepare follow the directions below.

1. Use standard half-pint canner-freezer jars with metal lids and screw bands. Thoroughly wash the jars and sterilize, then drain.

2. Prepare fruit and sugar mixture, following recipe instructions.

3. In a medium saucepan bring the pectin and the specified amount of water to a full rolling boil. Boil the mixture hard for 1 minute, stirring constantly. Remove the pan from the heat.

4. Stir boiling hot pectin into fruit-sugar mixture. Continue stirring for 3 minutes. Some sugar crystals may still remain.

5. Pour or ladle mixture into jars, filling to within ½ inch of the top. Do not use paraffin. Wipe sealing edge with a damp cloth. Cover with metal lids and tighten screw bands.

6. Let filled glasses stand 24 hours at room temperature to allow mixture to set up. (These products will be softer than cooked jams.)

7. Store these uncooked products in the freezer. After opening, store in the refrigerator and use within three weeks.

Sealing Cooked Jellies and Jams

Two types of sealing materials are suitable for sealing jars containing boiling hot jellies and jams. Use either paraffin or standard canning lids with metal screw bands. Naturally, the flat metal lids fit only standard canning jars, but paraffin can be used to seal any type of jelly glass.

Sealing with metal lids and screw bands:

1. Prepare the metal lids according to manufacturer's directions.

2. Place a wide-mouth funnel in the top of the jar, and carefully pour or ladle the hot mixture into the sterilized jars (photo A). Fill to within ½ inch of the top. Work quickly because the jelly will begin to set up.

3. As soon as the jars are filled, wipe the rims with a clean damp cloth or paper towel (photo B). This removes any trace of syrup or pieces of fruit from the sealing surface. Be sure to use a potholder, as the jars will be very hot. Work quickly.

4. Place metal lids on jars and tighten screw bands. Grasping the bottom of the jar firmly with a potholder, invert the jar for a few seconds so that the hot mixture is against the lid (photo C). The scalding hot jelly heats the lid and effectively sterilizes it. Then, turn the jar right-side up and allow jelly to cool on a rack placed out of a draft. Allow space between the jars for air circulation.

Place a funnel firmly in the mouth of a hot sterilized jar. Carefully ladle or pour the boiling jelly into the jar, filling to within ½ inch of the top.

After the jars are filled, take a damp cloth and wipe off sealing edge. Grasp hot jars with a potholder. Place lids on jars and tighten screw band.

5. When the jars are cool, check the seal by looking for the indentation in the center of the lid. Press the center of the lid with your fingertips. If indentation holds after you take your finger away, jar is sealed. Sealed jars are ready to label and store.

Sealing with paraffin:

1. Melt blocks of paraffin over hot water in an old double boiler or container that can be set over hot water. (Paraffin is highly flammable and should be handled with great care over low heat. The double boiler method of melting is the safest.)

2. Place a wide-mouth funnel in the top of the jar and carefully pour or ladle the hot mixture into hot sterilized jar (photo A) to within ½ inch of the top.

3. Spoon on *thin* layer of melted paraffin over the surface of the jelly or jam. This is to seal out the air (photo D). Grasp the hot jar with a potholder, and rotate it slowly so that the paraffin will cling to sides of the jelly glass above the surface of the jelly or jam. Prick any air bubbles that appear in the paraffin before they have time to set. After the paraffin has hardened, spoon on another *thin* layer of melted paraffin (total depth for both layers about ⅛ inch).

4. Let jars stand out of a draft until jelly is cool and paraffin has set. Wipe outside of jars with a damp cloth. Before storing, be sure there are no breaks in the set paraffin.

Causes of poor products

Cloudy jelly may be caused by:
Allowing jelly to stand before pouring.
Allowing pulp to go through jelly bag.
Using green fruit — jelly sets too fast.
Pouring the jelly mixture into the glasses too slowly.

Crystals in jelly are caused by:
Too much sugar.
Undercooking the mixture.
Overcooking or cooking too slowly.
Allowing jelly to stand, uncovered, after the jar is opened.

Weeping jelly usually results from:
Too thick a layer of paraffin on top.
Storing the jelly in a warm place.
Overcooking.
Too much pectin or acid.

Stiff or tough jelly is caused by:
Boiling the jelly too long.
Using too much additional pectin.

---

5. Label jars and cover tightly to prevent dust from settling on the paraffin. Commercial jelly glasses have colorful lids for this purpose, but foil or waxed paper anchored with string also works well. Store in cool place.

To complete the sealing of flat metal lids, turn the jars upside down. Hold long enough so that metal lid becomes hot. Turn jars right side up to cool.

Check the seal on cooled jellies before storing. Be sure there are no gaps in the paraffin. Look for the dip in the metal lid. Remove screw band.

APPLE JELLY

Tart apples contain enough natural pectin to make jelly gel, so you need not add commercial pectin. (When making this jelly, see photos on page 60.) —

  3 pounds tart apples (10 to 11 apples)
  Water
  3 cups sugar

Wash apples; remove blossom ends and stems. Do not peel or core. Cut apples into small chunks. In 8- to 10-quart kettle or Dutch oven combine apples and enough water to cover apples, about 5 cups. Cover and bring to boiling over high heat. Reduce heat; simmer just till apples are soft, 20 to 25 minutes.

Strain cooked apple and liquid through jelly bag; measure 4 cups juice. In 8- to 10-quart kettle or Dutch oven stir together apple juice and sugar till dissolved. Bring mixture to full rolling boil. Boil hard, uncovered, till syrup sheets off a metal spoon, 10 to 12 minutes.

Remove from heat; quickly skim off foam with metal spoon. Pour or ladle into hot sterilized jars; seal. Makes 3 half-pints.

FREEZER RASPBERRY JELLY

Next time, substitute fresh strawberries —

  2 quarts fully ripe red raspberries
  6 cups sugar
  1 1¾-ounce package powdered fruit
    pectin
  ¾ cup water

Wash and thoroughly crush the ripe raspberries. Strain raspberry juice through jelly bag (see photo B on page 60). Measure 3 cups raspberry juice into large mixing bowl. (If necessary, add water to make 3 cups.) Stir sugar into juice mixture; mix well.

In small saucepan combine powdered fruit pectin and ¾ cup water. Bring mixture to full rolling boil. Boil hard, uncovered, 1 minute, stirring constantly. Stir hot mixture into juice-sugar mixture; stir for 3 minutes. Pour at once into hot sterilized jars or freezer containers; seal. Let jelly stand at room temperature till set, about 24 hours. (Mixture will be softer than cooked jelly.)

Store jelly in refrigerator for up to 3 weeks or freeze. Makes 7 half-pints.

MINT-APPLE JELLY

  4 cups canned apple juice
  1 cup fresh mint leaves (lightly packed)
  1 1¾-ounce package powdered fruit
    pectin
  6 drops green food coloring
  4½ cups sugar

In 8- to 10-quart kettle or Dutch oven combine apple juice, mint, pectin, and food coloring. Bring mixture to full rolling boil. Stir in sugar. Bring again to full rolling boil; boil hard, uncovered, 1 minute, stirring constantly. Remove from heat. Remove mint. Quickly skim off foam with metal spoon. Pour at once into hot sterilized jars; seal. Makes 6 half-pints.

BASIL JELLY

  6½ cups sugar
  1 cup white vinegar
  1 cup basil leaves (lightly packed)
  6 drops green food coloring
  1 6-ounce bottle liquid fruit pectin

In 8- to 10-quart kettle or Dutch oven combine sugar, vinegar, basil, food coloring, and 2 cups water. Bring to boiling. Add pectin. Bring mixture to full rolling boil. Boil hard, uncovered, 1 minute, stirring constantly. Remove from heat. Remove basil. Quickly skim off foam with metal spoon. Pour at once into hot sterilized jars; seal. Makes 7 half-pints.

CRANBERRY JELLY

  3½ cups cranberry juice cocktail
  1 1¾-ounce package powdered fruit
    pectin
  4 cups sugar
  ¼ cup lemon juice

In 8- to 10-quart kettle or Dutch oven combine cranberry juice and pectin. Bring to full rolling boil. Stir in sugar. Bring again to full rolling boil. Boil hard, uncovered, 1 minute, stirring constantly. Remove from heat. Stir in lemon juice. Quickly skim off foam with metal spoon. Pour at once into hot sterilized jars; seal. Makes 6 half-pints.

ORANGE-SAUTERNE JELLY

4 cups sugar
1½ cups sauterne
1 teaspoon finely shredded orange peel
½ cup orange juice
2 tablespoons lemon juice
½ of a 6-ounce bottle liquid fruit pectin

In 8- to 10-quart kettle or Dutch oven combine sugar, sauterne, peel, orange juice, and lemon juice; mix well. Bring mixture to boiling. Reduce heat; simmer, uncovered, 2 minutes. Remove from heat; stir in pectin. Quickly skim off foam with metal spoon. Pour at once into hot sterilized jars; seal. Makes 4 half-pints.

CRAN-PINEAPPLE JELLY

3 cups cranberry juice cocktail
1 cup unsweetened pineapple juice
⅓ cup lemon juice
1 1¾-ounce package powdered fruit pectin
5 cups sugar

In 8- to 10-quart kettle or Dutch oven combine juices with pectin. Bring to full rolling boil, stirring constantly. Stir in sugar. Bring again to full rolling boil. Boil hard, uncovered, 1 minute, stirring constantly. Remove from heat; skim off foam. Pour at once into hot sterilized jars; seal. Makes 6 half-pints.

ORANGE-GRAPEFRUIT JELLY

3¼ cups sugar
1 cup water
3 tablespoons lemon juice
½ of a 6-ounce bottle liquid fruit pectin
1 6-ounce can frozen orange-grapefruit juice concentrate, thawed

In 8- to 10-quart kettle or Dutch oven combine sugar and water. Stirring constantly, bring mixture to full rolling boil. Add lemon juice. Boil hard, uncovered, 1 minute. Remove from heat. Stir in pectin and orange-grapefruit juice; mix well. Quickly skim off foam with metal spoon. Pour at once into hot sterilized jars; seal. Makes 5 half-pints.

Top off an early-morning breakfast or an extra-special Sunday brunch by serving golden Apple Marmalade *on hot muffins, biscuits, or toast.*

APPLE MARMALADE

1 orange
6 medium apples, peeled, cored, and coarsely chopped (6 cups)
3 tablespoons lemon juice
5 cups sugar

Quarter unpeeled orange. Remove seeds. Thinly slice orange. In 8- to 10-quart kettle or Dutch oven combine first three ingredients and 2 cups water. Bring mixture to boiling. Reduce heat; simmer till apples are tender, about 10 minutes. Add sugar. Bring to full rolling boil, stirring constantly. Continue cooking and stirring till thickened and clear (220° on candy thermometer). Remove from heat; skim off foam. Pour at once into hot sterilized jars; seal. Makes 6 half-pints.

CRAN-MARMALADE

2 12-ounce jars orange marmalade
16 ounces fresh cranberries, ground
2 cups sugar

In 8- to 10-quart kettle or Dutch oven combine all ingredients and 1 cup water. Bring to full rolling boil. Boil hard, uncovered, 5 minutes, stirring often. Remove from heat; quickly skim off foam with metal spoon. Pour at once into hot sterilized jars; seal. Makes 6 half-pints.

ORANGE MARMALADE

Remove peels from 4 medium oranges and 1 medium lemon; scrape off excess white. Cut peels into very fine strips. Add 1½ cups water and ¼ teaspoon baking soda. Bring to boiling; cover and simmer 10 minutes. Remove white membrane on fruit; section fruit, working over bowl to catch juice. Combine sections, juice, and undrained peel. Cover and simmer 20 minutes.

Measure 3 cups cooked fruit mixture; add 6 cups sugar. Bring to full rolling boil; boil, uncovered, 5 minutes. Remove from heat; stir in ½ of a 6-ounce bottle liquid fruit pectin. Skim off foam. Pour at once into hot sterilized jars; seal. Makes 6 half-pints.

CRANBERRY-PEAR MARMALADE

Remove peel from 1 lemon; scrape off excess white. Snip lemon peel into fine strips about 1 inch long. In 8- to 10-quart kettle or Dutch oven measure ¼ cup lemon peel and 2 tablespoons lemon juice. Add one 14-ounce jar cranberry-orange relish; 3 pears, peeled, cored, and ground; and 2 cups sugar.

Bring mixture to full rolling boil. Boil hard, uncovered, 5 minutes, stirring occasionally. Remove from heat; skim off foam with metal spoon. Pour at once into hot sterilized jars; seal. Makes about 3 half-pints.

TOMATO PRESERVES

  2 pounds ripe tomatoes, peeled, with stem
      ends and cores removed
  1 teaspoon grated lemon peel
  ¼ cup lemon juice
  6½ cups sugar
  1 6-ounce bottle liquid fruit pectin

Cut the peeled tomatoes in eighths or crush. In 8- to 10-quart kettle or Dutch oven measure 3 cups tomatoes. Simmer 10 minutes. Add peel and juice; stir in sugar.

Bring mixture to full rolling boil, stirring constantly. Boil hard, uncovered, 1 minute. Remove from heat; stir in pectin. Skim off foam with metal spoon. Pour at once into hot sterilized jars; seal. Makes 7 half-pints.

PEACH MARMALADE

  1 small orange
  1 lemon
  ¼ cup water
  3 pounds peaches
  1 1¾-ounce package powdered fruit
      pectin
  5 cups sugar

Cut orange and lemon in quarters; remove seeds. Slice orange and lemon quarters crosswise in paper-thin slices. In medium saucepan combine fruit slices and water. Cover and simmer the orange and lemon mixture 20 minutes. Peel, pit, and finely chop or grind peaches. In 8- to 10-quart kettle or Dutch oven combine orange and lemon mixture and chopped or ground peaches.

Stir pectin into fruit mixture. Bring mixture to full rolling boil. Stir in sugar; bring again to full rolling boil, stirring constantly. Boil hard, uncovered, 1 minute. Remove from heat; quickly skim off foam. Pour at once into hot sterilized jars; seal. Makes 7 or 8 half-pints.

WINTER PRESERVES

  1½ cups prunes
  1½ cups dried apricots
  5 cups water
  1 large orange
  5 cups sugar
  1 8¾-ounce can crushed pineapple

Rinse prunes and apricots. In medium saucepan cover fruit with water. Simmer mixture, covered, 15 minutes. Drain, reserving cooking liquid. Cool. Pit and cut up prunes. Cut up apricots. Peel orange, reserving peel. Section orange, working over bowl to catch juice. Dice orange sections. Scrape peel; discard white membrane. Slice peel into thin slivers.

In 8- to 10-quart kettle or Dutch oven combine prunes, apricots, reserved cooking liquid, orange peel, reserved orange juice, diced orange, sugar, and undrained pineapple. Boil mixture gently, uncovered, till of desired thickness, about 20 minutes. Stir occasionally. Remove from heat; quickly skim off foam with metal spoon. Pour at once into hot sterilized jars; seal. Makes 3 half-pints.

PEACH-CANTALOUPE CONSERVE

A refreshing fruit combination of sweet peaches and cantaloupe is captured in a tasty conserve —

>   3 cups chopped peaches (about 6 peaches)
>   3 cups chopped cantaloupe (1 medium cantaloupe)
>   4¼ cups sugar
>   3 tablespoons lemon juice
>
>   • • •
>
>   ⅓ cup slivered blanched almonds
>   ½ teaspoon ground nutmeg
>   ¼ teaspoon salt
>   ¼ teaspoon grated orange peel

In 8- to 10-quart kettle or Dutch oven mix peaches and cantalope. Bring mixture to full rolling boil; stir constantly. Add sugar and lemon juice. Bring mixture again to full rolling boil. Boil, uncovered, 12 minutes.

Add the slivered blanched almonds, nutmeg, salt, and grated orange peel. Boil hard, uncovered, till syrup sheets off metal spoon, 4 to 5 minutes. Remove from heat; quickly skim off foam with metal spoon. Pour at once into hot sterilized jars; seal. Makes 7 half-pints.

GRAPE CONSERVE

>   4 pounds Concord grapes
>   5 medium oranges
>   3 medium lemons
>   8 cups sugar
>   1 cup broken walnuts

Wash grapes. Separate skins from pulp; reserve grape skins. Cook pulp till soft; sieve to remove seeds. Squeeze oranges to measure 1½ cups juice; reserve peel from 2 oranges. Squeeze lemons to measure ½ cup juice; reserve peel from 1 lemon. Combine juices. Scrape excess white from peels. Slice peels very thin. Cover peels with water and cook, uncovered, till tender; drain. In 8- to 10-quart kettle or Dutch oven combine grape skins, grape pulp, fruit juices, peels, and sugar.

Bring to full rolling boil. Boil, uncovered, till mixture is thick and sheets off metal spoon, 35 to 40 minutes. Stir occasionally. Stir in walnuts. Remove from heat; quickly skim off foam with metal spoon. Pour at once into hot sterilized jars; seal. Makes 10 half-pints.

PLUM CONSERVE

>   2 pounds Italian plums
>   1 cup raisins
>   1 medium orange
>   3 cups sugar
>   ½ cup coarsely chopped walnuts

Pit the plums. Grind plums, raisins, and the orange. In 8- to 10-quart kettle or Dutch oven combine the ground fruit. Stir in the sugar. Bring mixture to full rolling boil. Cook, uncovered, till thick, about 10 minutes. Stir in the coarsely chopped walnuts.

Remove from heat; quickly skim off foam with metal spoon. Pour at once into hot sterilized jars; seal. Makes 6 half-pints.

FREEZER PINEAPPLE CONSERVE

Simplify the job of finely chopping a fresh pineapple by using your blender —

>   1 large fresh pineapple
>   1 teaspoon grated orange peel
>   ½ cup orange juice
>   Yellow food coloring (optional)
>   5 cups sugar
>   ½ cup chopped walnuts
>   ½ cup flaked coconut
>   ¾ cup water
>   1 1¾-ounce package powdered fruit pectin

Remove pineapple crown. Wash and peel pineapple; remove eyes and core. Cut into pieces. Place pineapple, a few pieces at a time, in blender container; cover and blend on low speed till finely chopped (not pureed). Measure 2 cups chopped pineapple. In large bowl combine pineapple, peel, orange juice, and several drops yellow food coloring, if desired.

Stir sugar, chopped walnuts, and flaked coconut into fruit mixture. In small saucepan combine water and the powdered fruit pectin. Bring the mixture to full rolling boil. Boil hard, uncovered, 1 minute, stirring constantly. Stir hot mixture into the fruit-sugar mixture, stirring 3 minutes. Pour at once into hot sterilized jars; seal. Let stand till set, about 24 hours. For use within 2 to 3 weeks, store conserve in refrigerator or freeze conserve up to 3 months. Makes 6 half-pints.

Sample these tasty jellies and jams: Cranberry Jelly *(page 65),* Strawberry Jam, Spiced Blueberry Jam, Sweet Cherry Jam, Pear-Peach Jam, *and* Freezer Strawberry Jam. *Each is delicious on hot bread.*

CHERRY-PEACH JAM

   1 pound tart red cherries
1¼ pounds peaches
   2 tablespoons lemon juice
   1 1¾-ounce package powdered fruit
      pectin
   4 cups sugar

Sort, wash, and remove the stems from red cherries. Pit and coarsely chop the cherries; measure 1½ cups. Peel, pit, and coarsely chop the peaches; measure 2 cups. In 8- to 10-quart kettle or Dutch oven combine the chopped fruit and lemon juice. Add the powdered fruit pectin to the mixture; mix well.

Bring mixture to full rolling boil. Stir in sugar. Bring again to full rolling boil, stirring constantly. Boil hard, uncovered, 1 minute. Remove from heat; quickly skim off foam with metal spoon. Pour at once into hot sterilized jars; seal. Makes 5 half-pints.

SPICED BLUEBERRY JAM

The spice is nice when ground cinnamon and cloves team with fresh blueberries —

   1 pound fully ripe blueberries
3½ cups sugar
   1 tablespoon lemon juice
  ¼ teaspoon ground cinnamon
  ⅛ teaspoon ground cloves
  ½ of a 6-ounce bottle liquid fruit pectin

Sort, wash, and remove any stems from the fresh blueberries. Crush the blueberries; measure 2½ cups. In 8- to 10-quart kettle or Dutch oven combine berries, sugar, lemon juice, ground cinnamon, and cloves.

Bring mixture to full rolling boil; boil hard, uncovered, 1 minute, stirring constantly. Remove from heat. Stir in liquid fruit pectin. Quickly skim off foam with a metal spoon. Pour hot jam at once into hot sterilized jars; seal. Makes 5 or 6 half-pints.

SWEET CHERRY JAM

Making a special homemade jam is an excellent way to preserve dark sweet cherries—

**1½ pounds fully ripe dark sweet cherries
2 cups sugar
2 tablespoons lemon juice**

Sort, wash, remove stems, and pit cherries; measure 3 cups. Cut up cherries. In 8- to 10-quart kettle or Dutch oven combine cherries and ¼ cup water. Bring to boil. Cover; simmer 15 minutes. Stir in sugar and juice; mix well.

Bring mixture to full rolling boil, stirring constantly. Boil, uncovered, till thick, 7 to 10 minutes. Remove from heat; quickly skim off foam with metal spoon. Pour at once into hot sterilized jars; seal. Makes 3 half-pints.

STRAWBERRY JAM

**2 quarts fresh strawberries
7 cups sugar
½ of a 6-ounce bottle liquid fruit pectin**

Wash berries. Slice in half lengthwise or quarter large berries; measure 4 cups. In 8- to 10-quart kettle or Dutch oven combine berries and *1 cup* sugar; let stand 15 minutes. Add remaining sugar. Bring to full rolling boil. Boil hard, uncovered, 1 minute, stirring constantly.

Remove from heat. Stir in pectin. Skim off foam with metal spoon. Pour at once into hot sterilized jars; seal. Makes 7 half-pints.

FREEZER STRAWBERRY JAM

**2 10-ounce packages frozen strawberries, thawed
3½ cups sugar
½ of a 6-ounce bottle liquid fruit pectin**

Mash berries or put through food mill. Add sugar; mix well. Let berries stand 20 minutes, stirring occasionally. When sugar has dissolved, add pectin and stir 3 minutes. Pour at once into hot sterilized jars or clean freezer containers; seal. Cover and let stand till set, about 24 hours. Store jam up to 6 weeks in the refrigerator or up to 1 year in the freezer. Makes 4 half-pints.

PEAR-PEACH JAM

**1 pound pears
1 pound peaches
2 tablespoons lemon juice
1 1¾-ounce package powdered fruit pectin
5½ cups sugar**

Peel, core, and grind or finely chop pears; measure 2 cups. Peel, pit, and grind or finely chop peaches; measure 2 cups. In 8- to 10-quart kettle or Dutch oven combine pears, peaches, lemon juice, and pectin.

Bring mixture to full rolling boil. Stir in sugar. Bring again to full rolling boil. Boil hard, uncovered, 1 minute, stirring constantly. Remove from heat; quickly skim off foam with metal spoon. Pour at once into hot sterilized jars; seal. Makes 7 half-pints.

APRICOT JAM

**3 pounds fully ripe apricots
⅓ cup water
3 cups sugar
2 tablespoons lemon juice**

Wash, peel, and pit apricots. Chop fruit and measure 4½ cups. In 8- to 10-quart kettle or Dutch oven combine apricots and water. Bring mixture to boiling. Cover and simmer apricots till tender, 5 to 10 minutes, stirring frequently. Add sugar and lemon juice; mix well. Stir until the sugar dissolves.

Bring fruit mixture to full rolling boil. Cook the jam till it is the desired thickness, 7 to 8 minutes, stirring constantly. Remove from heat; quickly skim off foam with metal spoon. Pour at once into hot sterilized jars; seal. Makes 6 half-pints.

RED PLUM JAM

Wash and pit 3 pounds red plums. Put through food chopper, using coarse blade; measure 5 cups. Add 4 cups sugar; let stand 1 hour. Boil hard, uncovered, till syrup sheets off metal spoon, 8 minutes. Remove from heat; quickly skim off foam. Pour at once into hot sterilized jars; seal. Makes 5 half-pints.

PICKLES AND RELISHES

Bring an extra measure of eating enjoyment to even the simplest fare by making and serving a variety of your family's favorite pickles and relishes. Pass a crisp dill pickle to munch with a noontime sandwich or salad. Complement an everyday meat loaf or Sunday dinner roast with a colorful spiced peach or a spoonful of peppy relish.

There is almost no limit to the solo vegetables, mixed vegetables, or fruits that can be turned into tantalizing pickles and relishes. Although categories overlap, pickles are usually grouped according to whether they are fermented in brine or packed with vinegar.

Brined or fermented pickles are made from vegetables, usually cucumbers, that are submerged in a brine solution and allowed to cure or ferment several days before canning. Dill, garlic, or other herbs or spices provide the special seasoning.

Fresh-pack pickles are made from vegetables or fruits, either whole or in pieces, that are canned in a spicy vinegar solution. Sometimes, a brine soaking period is used, but it is short—only a few hours or overnight. Sugar is added to the pickling solution when a sweeter product is desired.

Relishes are made from chopped vegetables or fruits that are cooked in a spicy vinegar solution to the desired consistency before canning. Relishes are sweet if sugar is added or hot if peppers or spices are included.

Pickling Basics

Pickling is one of the oldest methods of preserving food from one season to the next. Over the years, several pickle-making techniques have evolved. An early way was simply

Pickle a favorite relish

← *Colorful* Chowchow *(page 79), one of the all-time great relishes, combines cauliflower, corn, beans, onions, peppers, tomatoes, and spices. It's a delectable accompaniment for roast beef or ham.*

Process pickles and relishes

After packing your homemade pickles and relishes in standard canning jars, seal the jars and process in a waterbath canner. The processing destroys organisms that cause spoilage and ensures the keeping quality. You'll also be impressed with the good flavor at serving time. The necessary processing times are given for all pickle and relish recipes in this book.

---

to let the pickles cure or ferment in a concentrated salt solution. Later, the acid in vinegar was relied upon not only for flavor but also to preserve the vegetables. At various times, other ingredients such as slaked lime or powdered alum were added to the pickling solution to improve crispness of the products.

Today, water-bath canning is the important final step for successful pickles. (See tip box.)

The tart or sweet flavor and crisp texture of a good pickle are directly related to the quality of the ingredients and the way they are handled. The types of vegetables or fruits used and the proper balance of salt, vinegar, sugar, and water in the pickling liquid are important. So are the recipe directions and the equipment needed to carry them out.

Vegetables are the basis for most pickles and relishes. Choose only young tender produce for your pickle-making projects.

Cucumbers deserve special attention because they are probably the vegetable most often pickled. Whether you grow your own or buy them from a vegetable stand, choose a variety of cucumber that is developed just for pickling. Eating-type cucumbers do not make satisfactory pickles as a general rule. Sort the cucumbers according to the size needed for the recipe. Then, be sure that they are in the pickling solution within 24 hours after they have been picked.

Fruits make delicious pickles to serve with meat or poultry. Choose slightly underripe fruits and sort them for size according to the specific recipe. If the fruits are to be pickled whole, check the fruit carefully to detect bruises or cuts that will mar the attractiveness of the finished pickle.

Salt adds flavor and crispness to pickles. Use either pure granulated pickling salt or uniodized table salt. Pickling salt is preferred. Table salt, even the type without iodine, contains an anticaking ingredient that will make the brine cloudy. Do not use iodized table salt. It causes pickles to darken.

Vinegar provides the tartness in pickles and also acts as a preservative.

Choose a high-grade cider or white vinegar for your pickles. Cider vinegar has a pleasing flavor that blends well with the various herbs and spices in the pickling solution. Distilled white vinegar is slightly sharper. Use it to preserve the whiteness of vegetables such as cauliflower or pearl onions.

Vinegars are rated according to their acidity. For pickles always use one that is 4- to 6-percent acid. (This is sometimes stated as 40 to 60 grain.) The acidity is very important because pickles and relishes are made from low-acid vegetables. Never dilute the vinegar more than indicated in the recipe you are using. If you want a pickle with a milder flavor, add sugar to the pickling solution rather than dilute the vinegar.

Sugar balances the tartness of the vinegar. Check the recipe ingredient list to see whether to use granulated white sugar or packed brown sugar. White sugar is preferred for light-colored pickles. Brown sugar contributes a special flavor to darker varieties of pickles.

Water dissolves the salt and provides the liquid in a brine solution. Use soft water for preparing brine. If water in your area is naturally hard, boil it for 15 minutes, then let stand 24 hours. Carefully remove scum from top of water and dip water from kettle so as not to disturb the sediment in the bottom of the kettle. Add 1 tablespoon vinegar per gallon of boiled water before using.

Spices are the distinctive seasonings in pickles and relishes. Always use fresh herbs and spices to ensure maximum flavoring power. Often, you can tie whole spices in a piece of cheesecloth before adding to the pickling

---

Pickle pointers

- Select fresh, firm fruits and vegetables for pickling. Fruit is best if it is slightly underripe.
- Make pickles out of cucumbers within 24 hours of harvesting. Cucumbers that are held longer may produce a hollow or soft pickle.
- Use pure granulated pickling salt or uniodized table salt. Do not use iodized table salt. It causes pickles to darken.
- Choose a high-grade vinegar of 4- to 6-percent acid (40 to 60 grain). Use cider vinegar for most pickles, but substitute white vinegar when a light-colored product is desired.
- Add fresh herbs and spices. Spices deteriorate and lose strength quickly after the packages are opened.
- Use granulated white sugar unless brown sugar is specified in a recipe. Brown sugar produces a change in color and flavor in pickles.
- Use soft water for preparing brine for soaking or fermenting pickles. Minerals in hard water settle in the bottom of the jar after processing.
- Choose utensils made of stoneware, aluminum, glass, or stainless steel.

---

liquid. Remove the spice bag from the boiling liquid before filling the jars.

Dill is the best known of the herbs for pickles, but combinations of basil, marjoram, and thyme are often used, too. Spices such as peppercorns, allspice, turmeric, cloves, and stick cinnamon are important in pickle-making as are commercial mixed pickling spices.

Equipment and utensils needed for pickle-making are minimal. The biggest item is the water-bath canner with a rack. Standard canning jars with lids, one or more large pans or kettles and small kitchen tools complete the list of necessary equipment.

If you do other canning, you already have the water-bath canner. However, since pickles and relishes are canned in small jars, you can successfully use any large kettle deep enough to hold the jars and still have room for at least

1 inch of water to boil over the tops of the jars. Improvise a rack or buy one in a housewares department that will fit the kettle you plan to use for processing pickles.

Use standard canning jars and lids for packing pickles and relishes. They are the most satisfactory for water-bath processing.

Choose containers made from glass or stoneware for soaking pickles in brine. Enamelware containers can be used if there are no chipped places on them. Use aluminum, stainless steel, glass, or chip-free enamel kettles for heating the pickling liquid. Stir the pickling solution with wooden or stainless steel spoons. *Do not use copper, brass, chipped enamelware, galvanized, or iron utensils*. The material in the containers is important because you are working with acids and salts that can react with the metals on the do-not-use list to produce poisonous compounds.

Packing

1. Wash and rinse jars. Pour boiling water over them and allow them to stand in hot water till time to fill. Prepare lids according to manufacturer's directions.

2. Set water-bath canner containing a rack on your kitchen range. Fill the kettle with four to five inches of water. Place a cover on the canner and start heating the water over high heat. At the same time start heating water in another container to fill the canner after the jars are in place.

3. Pack the pickles or relish into prepared jars according to directions in the recipe, leaving ½-inch headspace. Put a cloth under the jar to prevent the jar from slipping and to catch any spills. A wide-mouth funnel will make it a great deal easier for you to fill the canning jars with relish or with pickle slices.

4. Spoon boiling pickling liquid over the food, leaving ½-inch headspace. The jar will get hot, so use a potholder.

5. Use a flexible spatula or table knife to work out any air bubbles in the filled canning jar. Move the spatula or knife around gently so as not to cut the pickles.

6. Wipe off the rim of the filled jar with a damp cloth or paper towel. This removes any trace of pickling liquid or bit of food or spice that could interfere with the proper sealing of the canning jar.

7. Put all the prepared lids on filled jars.

Zinc cap with rubber ring: Slip a wet flexible rubber ring over the mouth of the jar and fit it against the shoulder of the jar. Screw the cap down firmly against the rubber, then unscrew it about ¼ inch.

Metal lid with screw band: Place the lid, compound side down, on the rim of the jar. Add the metal band and screw down firmly. Do not loosen metal band.

8. By now, the water in the canner should be hot. Place filled jars on rack in canner, making sure the jars do not touch.

9. When the last jar has been added to the water-bath canner, check the water level. Using additional boiling water, fill the canner so that the water is at least one inch over the tops of the jars.

Processing

1. Count the processing time as follows:

Fermented pickles, or relishes and fresh-pack dill pickles. Start counting as soon as the jars are placed in the canner and the hot water covers them. Do not wait for water to return to boiling.

Fresh-pack pickles. Allow hot water covering jars in canner to return to a boil before starting to count processing time.

2. Remember that the times listed in each recipe are for pickles and relishes canned at sea level. Altitude above sea level will affect the timing that is needed for processing. Add 1 minute to the processing time for each 1,000 feet above sea level.

3. When processing time is up, turn heat off under canner and transfer the jars to a rack or folded towel in a draft-free area. Tighten zinc caps, if used. Leave space between the jars for the air to circulate.

Storing

1. After jars have cooled, check each jar to be sure it has sealed. Turn upside down those closed with zinc caps. If there is any leakage, reseal and process again. For metal lids with screw bands, look for the indentation in the center of the lids. Remove screw band.

2. Wipe jars with a clean, damp cloth and label with product name and date. Store in a cool, dark place.

PICKLED BEETS

> 3 pounds small whole beets*
> 2 cups vinegar
> 1 cup water
> ½ cup sugar
> 1 teaspoon whole allspice
> 6 whole cloves
> 3 inches stick cinnamon

Wash beets, leaving on root and 1 inch of tops. Cover beets with boiling water; simmer 25 minutes. Drain. Slip off skins and trim beets. In large kettle combine vinegar, water, and sugar. Tie allspice, cloves, and cinnamon in cheesecloth bag. Add spice bag to pickling liquid. Bring to boiling; simmer 15 minutes. Pack beets into hot jars, leaving ½-inch headspace. Cover beets with boiling pickling liquid, leaving ½-inch headspace. Adjust lids. Process in boiling water bath (half-pints) 30 minutes. Makes 3 half-pints.

*For large beets, wash, remove tops, and cook as directed. Slip off skins; cube.

SWEET PICKLED CARROTS

Peel 6 pounds medium carrots (about 36). Cut lengthwise into quarters. Cook the carrots in boiling, salted water just till tender, 7 to 8 minutes; drain. In 8- to 10-quart kettle or Dutch oven combine 3 cups sugar, 3 cups vinegar, 3 cups water, ⅓ cup mustard seed, 6 inches stick cinnamon, and 6 whole cloves.

Bring to boiling; simmer 20 minutes. Pack carrots into hot jars, leaving ½-inch headspace. Cover with vinegar mixture, leaving ½-inch headspace. Adjust lids. Process in boiling water bath (pints) 5 minutes. Makes 6 pints.

Pickle problems

Shriveled pickles are produced by using too strong a salt, sugar, or vinegar solution; overcooking; or overprocessing.
Soft pickles are the result of using too little salt or acid, insufficient processing, or not fresh cucumbers.

PICKLED MUSHROOMS AND ONIONS

A must for mushroom lovers—

> 1 pound fresh whole mushrooms
> 2 medium onions, thinly sliced and
>   separated into rings (1 cup)
> 1½ cups red wine vinegar
> 1½ cups water
> ½ cup packed brown sugar
> 4 teaspoons pickling salt
> 1 teaspoon dried tarragon, crushed

Thoroughly wash the mushrooms; trim stems. In 3-quart saucepan combine onion rings, red wine vinegar, water, brown sugar, pickling salt, and the tarragon; bring the mixture to boiling. Add the mushrooms; simmer, uncovered, 5 minutes. Lift the mushrooms and onion rings from the pickling liquid with slotted spoon. Reserve the liquid; keep hot.

Pack the vegetables in hot jars, leaving ½-inch headspace. Cover with boiling pickling liquid leaving ½-inch headspace. Adjust lids. Process in boiling water bath (half-pints and pints) 5 minutes. Makes 4 half-pints.

PICKLED SWEET RED PEPPERS

> 2½ pounds sweet red peppers
> 2 cups sugar
> 2 cups tarragon vinegar
> 2 cups water
> ½ teaspoon celery seed
> ½ teaspoon mustard seed
> 2 cloves garlic, crushed
> 1 teaspoon salt

Thoroughly wash the red peppers. Remove tops and seeds from the peppers. Cut in quarters or sixths lengthwise, or in strips. In medium saucepan cook red peppers 3 minutes in boiling water. Drain peppers. In 6- to 8-quart kettle or Dutch oven combine sugar, tarragon vinegar, 2 cups water, celery seed, mustard seed, garlic, and salt.

Bring the mixture to boiling; simmer 5 minutes. Pack hot peppers into hot wide-mouth jars, leaving ½-inch headspace. Cover with boiling pickling liquid, leaving ½-inch headspace. Adjust lids. Process in boiling water bath (pints) 10 minutes. Makes 4 pints.

Home-canned Pickled Beets, Crisp Pickle Slices *(page 77),* Pickled Dilled Beans, Pickled Onions, Pickled Sweet Red Peppers, *and* Pickled Mushrooms and Onions *are all flavorful highlights with any meal.*

PICKLED DILLED BEANS

>   2 pounds green beans
>   1 cup white vinegar
>   2 tablespoons pickling salt
>   2 teaspoons dillweed
>   ¼ teaspoon cayenne
>   2 cloves garlic, crushed

Wash beans; drain. Trim ends. Cut beans to fit jars. Cover beans with boiling water; cook 3 minutes. Drain. Pack lengthwise into hot jars, leaving ½-inch headspace. In a saucepan combine vinegar, 3 cups water, pickling salt, dillweed, cayenne, and garlic; bring to boiling. Cover beans with pickling liquid, leaving ½-inch headspace. Adjust lids. Process in boiling water bath (pints and quarts) 10 minutes. Makes 4 pints.

PICKLED ONIONS

>   1½ pounds pearl onions
>   2 tablespoons pickling salt
>   1½ cups white vinegar
>   ⅓ cup sugar
>   1 teaspoon mixed pickling spices

Drop onions in boiling water to cover; boil 3 minutes. Drain; place in cold water. Cut root end; squeeze stem end to remove onion skin. Combine 2 cups water and pickling salt; pour over onions. Let stand 12 hours. Drain; rinse thoroughly. Combine vinegar, sugar, and pickling spices; bring to boiling. Pack onions into hot jars, leaving ½-inch headspace. Cover with pickling liquid, leaving ½-inch headspace. Adjust lids. Process in boiling water bath (half-pints) 10 minutes. Makes 4 half-pints.

WATERMELON PICKLES

2 pounds watermelon rind
¼ cup pickling salt
4 cups water
2 cups sugar
1 cup white vinegar
1 tablespoon broken stick cinnamon
1½ teaspoons whole cloves
½ lemon, thinly sliced
5 maraschino cherries, halved (optional)

Trim the dark green and pink parts from watermelon rind. Cut rind in 1-inch cubes; measure 7 cups. Soak rind overnight in a solution of pickling salt and water. (If it takes more to cover, use same proportion salt to water.) Drain; rinse watermelon rind. Cover rind with cold water. Cook just till tender.

Meanwhile, in 6- to 8-quart kettle or Dutch oven combine sugar, white vinegar, stick cinnamon, whole cloves, and 1 cup water. Simmer mixture 10 minutes; strain. Add drained watermelon rind, lemon slices, and maraschino cherries, if desired. Simmer the mixture till watermelon rind is clear. Fill hot jars with rind and syrup mixture, leaving ½-inch headspace. Adjust lids. Process in boiling water bath (pints) 5 minutes. Makes 2½ pints.

PICKLED ARTICHOKE HEARTS

4 pounds small artichokes
4 cups white vinegar
1 cup white wine vinegar
1 clove garlic, crushed
1 tablespoon salt

Wash artichokes. Cut off stem and ½ inch from top. Pull off coarser outer leaves. In 8- to 10-quart kettle or Dutch oven bring 4 cups white vinegar and 4 quarts water to boiling; add artichokes. Cover; simmer till leaf pulls off easily, about 10 minutes. Drain.

Cut artichokes in half; remove choke. Combine 4 cups water, wine vinegar, garlic, and salt to make brine. Bring to boiling. Pack artichoke hearts into hot jars, leaving ½-inch headspace. Pour boiling hot brine over artichokes, leaving ½-inch headspace; seal. Adjust lids. Process in boiling water bath (pints) 15 minutes. Makes 6 pints.

SWEET PICKLES

9½ pounds of 3- to 4-inch cucumbers
    (about 150)
1 cup pickling salt
12 cups sugar
8 cups cider vinegar
1 cup prepared horseradish
16 inches stick cinnamon
1½ teaspoons celery seed

Wash cucumbers; cover with hot brine made from pickling salt and 2 quarts boiling water. Cool; cover with plate or lid with weight atop to keep cucumbers in brine. Let stand 7 days.

Drain. Cover cucumbers with hot water; let stand 24 hours. Drain. Again cover with hot water; let stand 24 hours. Drain; split cucumbers in half. Combine sugar, cider vinegar, horseradish, cinnamon, and celery seed. Bring mixture to boiling. Slowly pour boiling syrup over cucumbers. Drain syrup from the cucumbers each morning for 4 days; reheat the syrup and pour over cucumbers. Let the cucumbers cool in the syrup before covering.

When you're ready to process, remove stick cinnamon and bring the cucumbers and syrup to boiling. Pack hot into hot jars, leaving ½-inch headspace. Cover the cucumbers with boiling hot syrup, leaving ½-inch headspace. Adjust lids. Process in boiling water bath (pints) 5 minutes. Makes 13 pints.

GREEN TOMATO DILL PICKLES

5 pounds small firm green tomatoes
Fresh dill heads *or* dillseed
Garlic cloves
Whole cloves
4 cups vinegar
⅓ cup salt

Wash tomatoes; slice ¼ inch thick. Pack tomatoes loosely into hot quart jars, leaving ½-inch headspace. To each quart add 3 or 4 heads dill or 2 tablespoons dillseed, 1 clove garlic, and 1 whole clove. In saucepan combine vinegar, salt, and 4 cups water. Bring to boiling.

Slowly pour boiling pickling liquid over tomatoes, leaving ½-inch headspace. Adjust lids. Process in boiling water bath (quarts) 20 minutes. Makes 5 quarts.

SWEET-SOUR PICKLES

3½ pounds of 2½-inch cucumbers (about 50)
½ cup pickling salt
6 cups cider vinegar
3 cups sugar
1 tablespoon mixed pickling spices

Wash cucumbers. Dissolve salt in 4 cups boiling water. In large bowl pour brine over cucumbers. Let stand in brine till cool; drain. Combine vinegar, sugar, pickling spices, and 2 cups water; bring to boiling. Slowly pour liquid over cucumbers; let stand 24 hours.

Bring cucumbers and pickling liquid to boiling. Pack cucumbers and pickling liquid into hot jars, leaving ½-inch headspace. Adjust lids. Process in boiling water bath (pints) 5 minutes. Makes 5 pints.

KOSHER DILL PICKLES

2½ pounds 4-inch cucumbers (about 25)
Fresh dill heads
Garlic cloves
Hot red peppers
Pickling salt
4 cups cider vinegar

Thoroughly wash cucumbers. Pack cucumbers in hot quart jars, leaving ½-inch headspace. To each quart add 2 heads fresh dill, 1 clove garlic, 1 hot pepper, and 1 tablespoon pickling salt. In medium saucepan combine vinegar and 3 quarts water. Bring mixture to boiling.

Slowly pour boiling hot pickling liquid over cucumbers, leaving ½-inch headspace. Adjust lids. Process in boiling water bath (quarts) 20 minutes. Makes about 5 quarts.

DILL PICKLES

Wash 3- or 4-inch cucumbers. Pack loosely into hot jars, leaving ½-inch headspace. To each quart add 3 or 4 heads fresh dill and 1 teaspoon mustard seed. For each quart combine 2 cups water, 1 cup vinegar, and 1 tablespoon pickling salt; bring to boiling. Slowly pour hot pickling liquid over the cucumbers, leaving ½-inch headspace. Adjust lids. Process in boiling water bath (quarts) 20 minutes.

CRISP PICKLE SLICES

4 quarts sliced unpeeled medium
    cucumbers
6 medium white onions, sliced (6 cups)
2 green peppers, sliced (1⅔ cups)
3 cloves garlic
⅓ cup pickling salt
    Cracked ice
5 cups sugar
3 cups cider vinegar
2 tablespoons mustard seed
1½ teaspoons turmeric
1½ teaspoons celery seed

Combine cucumbers, onions, green pepper, garlic, and salt. Cover with cracked ice; mix well. Let mixture stand 3 hours; drain well. Remove garlic. Combine remaining ingredients; pour over cucumber mixture. Bring to boiling. Pack cucumbers and liquid into hot jars, leaving ½-inch headspace. Adjust lids. Process in boiling water bath (half-pints or pints) 5 minutes. Makes 8 pints.

CORN AND TOMATO RELISH

½ cup sugar
1 tablespoon turmeric
2 16-ounce cans whole kernel corn,
    drained (4 cups)
1 16-ounce can tomatoes, cut up (2 cups)
2 cups chopped onion
2 cups chopped, peeled cucumber
2 cups chopped green pepper
1 cup chopped celery
2 dried small hot red peppers, seeded
    and crushed (optional)
1 cup vinegar
2 teaspoons mustard seed
2 tablespoons cornstarch

In 8- to 10-quart kettle or Dutch oven combine sugar, 2 tablespoons salt, and turmeric. Add vegetables, vinegar, and mustard seed; bring to boiling. Reduce heat; simmer, uncovered, 30 to 40 minutes. Stir ¼ cup cold water into cornstarch; blend well. Add to vegetables; cook and stir till slightly thickened, about 5 minutes.

Ladle mixture into hot jars, leaving ½-inch headspace. Adjust lids. Process in boiling water bath (pints) 15 minutes. Makes 4½ pints.

RED PEPPER RELISH

24 sweet red peppers, halved and seeded
7 medium onions, halved
3 cups sugar
3 cups vinegar
2 tablespoons salt

Thinly slice peppers and onions, or use a coarse blade to grind peppers and onions, reserving vegetable juices. In 4- to 6-quart kettle or Dutch oven combine reserved vegetable juices, peppers, onions, sugar, vinegar, and salt. Bring to boil; reduce heat and simmer mixture 30 minutes. Pour into hot jars, leaving ½-inch headspace. Adjust lids. Process in boiling water bath (half-pints) 15 minutes. Makes 10 half-pints.

BEET RELISH

4 pounds beets, cooked and peeled
4 large onions
3 large green peppers
1 tablespoon whole cloves
1½ cups sugar
1½ cups vinegar

Grind beets, onions, and green peppers. Tie cloves in cheesecloth bag. In large kettle combine vegetables, clove bag, sugar, vinegar, ½ cup water, and 1 tablespoon salt. Bring to boil; reduce heat. Cover; simmer 20 minutes, stirring occasionally. Remove clove bag. Ladle into hot jars; leave ½-inch headspace. Adjust lids. Process in boiling water bath (half-pints) 15 minutes. Makes 13 half-pints.

Delicious home-canned pickles, marmalades, and relishes make a perfect accompaniment. Pictured below: Sweet Pickled Carrots *(page 74),* Cran-Marmalade *(page 65),* Carrot-Cuke Relish *and* Red Pepper Relish.

CORN RELISH

  16 to 20 ears fresh corn
   4 cups chopped celery
   2 cups chopped sweet red pepper
   2 cups chopped green pepper
   1 cup chopped onion
   2 cups sugar
   2 cups vinegar
   2 teaspoons celery seed
   ¼ cup all-purpose flour
   2 tablespoons dry mustard
   1 teaspoon turmeric

Husk and silk corn. Cook in boiling water 5 minutes; plunge into cold water. Drain. Cut corn from cobs; do not scrape cobs. Measure 8 cups cut corn. In 8- to 10-quart kettle or Dutch oven combine celery, red pepper, green pepper, and onion. Add sugar, vinegar, celery seed, 2 cups water, and 2 tablespoons salt. Bring vegetable mixture to boiling. Boil, uncovered, 5 minutes, stirring occasionally.

Blend flour, dry mustard, and turmeric with ½ cup cold water. Add along with corn to boiling mixture. Return to boiling; cook and stir 5 minutes. Pack loosely into hot jars, leaving ½-inch headspace. Adjust lids. Process in boiling water bath (pints) 15 minutes. Makes 7 pints.

CARROT-CUKE RELISH

   4 to 6 unpeeled cucumbers, coarsely
        ground (3½ cups)
   6 medium carrots, coarsely ground
        (1½ cups)
   2 medium onions, coarsely ground (1 cup)
   2 tablespoons salt
   2 cups sugar
   1½ cups vinegar
   1½ teaspoons celery seed
   1½ teaspoons mustard seed

Combine ground vegetables and salt. Let stand 3 hours; drain. In 8- to 10-quart kettle or Dutch oven combine sugar, vinegar, celery seed, and mustard seed; bring to boiling. Add vegetables. Bring to boiling; reduce heat and simmer 20 minutes. Ladle mixture into hot jars, leaving ½-inch headspace. Adjust lids. Process in boiling water bath (half-pints) 15 minutes. Makes 5 half-pints.

CHOWCHOW

   3 large onions
   5 green tomatoes, stem ends removed
   6 green peppers
   2 cups green beans cut in ½-inch pieces
   2 cups cauliflower broken into
        small buds
   2 cups fresh corn kernels
   ¼ cup pickling salt
   3 cups sugar
   2 cups vinegar
   1 tablespoon mustard seed
   1½ teaspoons celery seed
   ¾ teaspoon turmeric

Using coarse blade of food grinder, grind onions, tomatoes, and green peppers. In large bowl combine ground vegetables, beans, cauliflower, and corn. Sprinkle with pickling salt; let stand overnight. Rinse and drain. Combine sugar, vinegar, mustard seed, celery seed, turmeric, and 1 cup water; pour over vegetables. Bring to boiling; boil gently 5 minutes. Ladle into hot jars, leaving ½-inch headspace. Adjust lids. Process in boiling water bath (pints) 15 minutes. Makes about 6 pints.

VEGETABLE RELISH

   5 cups ground green peppers (12 peppers)
   4 cups ground green tomatoes
        (10 tomatoes)
   4 cups ground onions (7 large)
   4 cups ground cabbage (1 medium head)
   1½ cups ground sweet red peppers
        (6 peppers)
   ½ cup pickling salt
   6 cups sugar
   4 cups cider vinegar
   2 cups water
   2 tablespoons mustard seed
   1 tablespoon celery seed
   1½ teaspoons turmeric

In bowl combine vegetables and pickling salt; let stand overnight. Thoroughly rinse and drain. Combine remaining ingredients; pour over vegetables. Bring to boil; boil gently 5 minutes. Ladle into hot jars; leave ½-inch headspace. Adjust lids. Process in boiling water bath (half-pints or pints) 15 minutes. Makes 9 pints.

Keeping the freezer full is the secret to making it work for you year-round. Figure out what foods are the most important for the space available. Then, plan ahead to save money on seasonal produce and specials on meats. For example, some families count on a garden to fill the freezer in the fall and later buy a quarter of beef from a locker plant. Others buy the produce from a market and pick up steaks and roasts at the meat counter. Whatever the supply, complete directions for freezing each item are in this chapter.

Freezing Know-How

Become familiar with the types of containers and wrapping materials available for freezing foods. Learn how to wrap each properly to eliminate air and to prevent freezer burn. Pay particular attention to the storage time charts for each type of food. Once foods are in the freezer, you can rotate packages and use them within the recommended storage time.

Fill the extra freezer spaces with baked products, main dishes, or desserts. Discover how to double a favorite recipe, serving one now and wrapping and freezing the other for use later. Or, wrap and freeze leftovers for another meal.

A supply of juicy Strawberries *(page 84) in the freezer ensures plenty of good eating in the months ahead. Spoon berries over breakfast food, or layer with ice cream for a dinner parfait.*

FRUITS

Most fruits, except bananas, freeze satisfactorily. When prepared properly, they retain fresh flavor, bright natural color, and nutritive value. Follow these simple directions:

1. Select the same fresh, ripe fruit you would choose for eating (see chart). Wash the fruit carefully in cold water; drain well.

2. Follow the charts on pages 83 and 84 for preparing and packing fruits with sugar or syrup. Use the syrup proportions at the right for making the syrup. If you prefer fruits without sugar or syrup, use the unsweetened fruit pack, also at the right.

3. Pack fruit tightly in moisture-vaporproof containers to eliminate air. Allow space at top, as food will expand during freezing. The amount of headspace needed differs, depending on the type of pack and the size of the container being used.

Liquid or semiliquid pack: For wide-top pints leave ½-inch headspace; wide-top quarts, 1 inch. For narrow-top pints leave ¾-inch headspace; narrow-top quarts, 1½ inches.

Dry pack: Allow ½-inch headspace for all sizes of freezer containers.

4. Keep floating fruits that tend to darken below the syrup by placing crumpled parchment paper, crushed plastic wrap, or waxed paper atop fruit in container.

5. Follow manufacturer's directions for sealing. Label with contents and date.

6. Freeze promptly and store at 0° or below. Frozen fruits may be stored for 8 to 12 months. Do not refreeze thawed fruits.

SYRUP PROPORTIONS

Light Syrup: 2 cups sugar and 4 cups boiling water yield 5 cups syrup.

Medium Syrup: 3 cups sugar and 4 cups boiling water yield 5½ cups syrup.

Heavy Syrup: 4¾ cups sugar and 4 cups boiling water yield 6½ cups syrup.

Very Heavy Syrup: 7 cups sugar and 4 cups boiling water yield 7¾ cups syrup. Stir to dissolve sugar. Chill. Figure ½ to ⅔ cup of syrup for each pint of fruit.

UNSWEETENED FRUIT PACK

Apples: Wash, peel, and core. Dissolve ½ teaspoon ascorbic acid color keeper in 1 quart water. Pour ½ cup of this water into a freezer container. Slice apples into container. Press down; cover with water. Leave ½-inch headspace. Seal; label; freeze.

Blueberries: Wash; drain. Steam 1 minute; cool quickly. Pack; cover with cold water. Leave ½-inch headspace. Seal; label; freeze.

Peaches or Strawberries: Wash. Cut as desired. Pack; cover with water containing 1 teaspoon ascorbic acid color keeper per quart. Leave ½-inch headspace in pints; 1-inch headspace in quarts. Seal; label; freeze.

Plums or Raspberries: Wash. Pack whole; leave ½-inch headspace. Seal; label; freeze.

Rhubarb: Wash, trim, and cut into 1- or 2-inch pieces or in lengths to fit container. Cook in boiling water 1 minute; cool quickly in cold water. Pack; cover with cold water. Leave ½-inch headspace. Seal; label; freeze.

Frozen fruit yield

Generally, the following amount of fruit as purchased yields 1 pint frozen fruit.

Fruit	Amount
Apples	1¼ to 1½ pounds
Apricots	⅔ to ¾ pound
Berries*	1⅓ to 1½ pints
Peaches	1 to 1½ pounds
Pears	1 to 1¼ pounds
Plums	1 to 1½ pounds
Raspberries	1 pint
Rhubarb	⅔ to 1 pound
Strawberries	⅔ quart

*Blackberries, blueberries, boysenberries, elderberries, loganberries.

Selecting Fruits for Freezing

Use only high-quality fruits for freezing. Firm, vine- or tree-ripened fruit is the most satisfactory. Select fruit that is slightly riper than that used for canning but is not soft or mushy. Unripe fruit, which is hard and immature, lacks flavor after it has been frozen. Ripe fruit just right for eating may be your best guide for selecting fruits for freezing. Eating-ripe fruit has as its characteristics firm texture, good color, and full flavor.

Apples	Ripe, firm, full-flavored, crisp
Apricots	Fully ripe, firm, plump, golden yellow color
Blueberries	Ripe, full-flavored, large, dark blue color with soft, powdery bloom
Cherries	Tree-ripened, firm, bright red
Peaches	Ripe, moderately firm to the touch, creamy to yellow background color
Pears	Fairly firm to touch, yet beginning to soften, shiny skin
Plums	Ripe, slightly soft to touch, well-colored for variety
Raspberries	Fully ripened, firm, juicy, purple or red better than black for freezing
Rhubarb	Firm, tender, glossy stalk with large amount of pink or red color
Strawberries	Ripe, firm, red, fragrant aroma, stem caps attached

Freezing Fruits

Fruit	Syrup Pack	Sugar Pack
Apples	Wash, peel, and core. Add ½ teaspoon ascorbic acid color keeper per quart Medium Syrup. In container slice apples into ½ cup cold syrup. Press down; cover with syrup; leave headspace. Seal.	Wash, peel, core, and slice. Steam 1½ to 2 minutes. Cool; drain. Sprinkle ½ cup sugar over each quart of fruit; stir. Pack tightly into containers, leaving headspace. Seal; label; freeze.
Apricots	Wash, halve, and pit. Peel and slice. If not peeled, cook in boiling water ½ minute. Cool; drain. Add ¾ teaspoon ascorbic acid color keeper to each quart Medium Syrup. Pack fruit tightly into containers. Cover with cold syrup; leave headspace. Seal; label; freeze.	Wash, halve, and pit. Peel, if desired. If not peeled, cook in boiling water ½ minute. Cool; drain. Dissolve ¼ teaspoon ascorbic acid color keeper in ¼ cup cold water; sprinkle over 1 quart apricots. Mix ½ cup sugar with each quart fruit; stir till dissolved. Pack, pressing down till juice covers fruit. Leave headspace. Seal.
Blueberries Elderberries Huckleberries	Wash; drain. Steam 1 minute; cool quickly. Pack into containers; cover with cold Medium Syrup. Leave headspace. Seal; label; freeze.	Wash; drain. Steam 1 minute; cool. To 1 quart berries, add ⅔ cup sugar; mix. Place the berries in containers; leave headspace. Seal; label; and freeze.

Freezing Fruits (continued)

Fruit	Syrup Pack	Sugar Pack
Cherries, sour	Stem, wash, drain, and pit. Pack into containers; cover with cold Heavy or Very Heavy Syrup. Leave headspace. Seal; label; freeze.	Stem, wash, drain, and pit. To each quart fruit add ¾ cup sugar; mix till dissolved. Pack into containers, leaving headspace. Seal; label; freeze.
Cherries, sweet	Stem, wash, and pit. Add ½ teaspoon ascorbic acid color keeper to each quart Medium Syrup. Pack into containers. Cover with syrup; leave headspace. Seal; label; freeze.	
Melons	Halve, remove seeds, and peel. Cut as desired; pack into containers. Cover with cold Light Syrup; leave headspace. Seal; label; freeze.	
Peaches	Wash; pit; peel (for smooth look, don't scald). Add ½ teaspoon ascorbic acid color keeper per quart Medium Syrup. In container slice into ½ cup syrup, or leave in halves; press down. Cover with syrup; leave headspace. Seal; label; freeze.	Wash, pit, and peel (for smooth look, don't scald). Halve or slice. Dissolve ¼ teaspoon ascorbic acid color keeper in ¼ cup cold water. Sprinkle over 1 quart fruit. Add ⅔ cup sugar; mix well. Pack into containers; leave headspace. Seal; label; freeze.
Pears	Wash, peel, halve or quarter, and core. Cook in boiling Medium Syrup 1 to 2 minutes. Drain; cool. Pack into containers. Add ¾ teaspoon ascorbic acid color keeper per quart syrup. Cover fruit with syrup; leave headspace. Seal; label; freeze.	
Plums	Wash, pit, and halve or quarter; pack into containers. Add ½ teaspoon ascorbic acid color keeper to each quart Medium or Heavy Syrup. Cover with syrup; leave headspace. Seal; label; freeze.	Wash, pit, and halve or quarter. To 1 pound fruit add ⅔ cup sugar; mix. Place in containers; leave headspace. Seal; label; freeze.
Raspberries Blackberries Boysenberries Strawberries	Wash and hull; slice, if desired. Place in containers. Cover with cold Medium or Heavy Syrup; leave headspace. Seal; label; freeze.	Wash and drain. Remove hulls and slice or leave whole. Add ¾ cup sugar to each quart berries; mix carefully. Place in containers; leave headspace. Seal; label; freeze.
Rhubarb	Wash, trim, and cut into 1- or 2-inch pieces. Cook in boiling water 1 minute; cool in cold water. Pack. Cover with cold Medium Syrup; leave headspace. Seal; label; freeze.	

VEGETABLES

Frozen vegetable yield

Generally, the following amount of vegetable as purchased yields 1 pint frozen.

Vegetable	Pounds
Asparagus	1 to 1½
Beans, limas in pods	2 to 2½
Beans, snap green	⅔ to 1
Beets, without tops	1¼ to 1½
Broccoli	1
Brussels sprouts	1
Carrots, without tops	1¼ to 1½
Cauliflower	1⅓
Corn, sweet in husks	2 to 2½
Peas	2 to 2½
Spinach	1 to 1½
Squash, summer	1 to 1¼
Squash, winter	1½
Sweet potatoes	⅔

Some vegetables freeze better than others. Those that lose their crispness and do not freeze well include salad greens, celery, green onion, cucumber, radishes, and tomatoes. Prepare vegetables for freezing as follows:

1. Select fresh, tender, ripe vegetables.

2. Wash, trim, and sort vegetables according to size, following charts on pages 86 and 87.

3. Blanch or scald vegetables in hot water to stop enzyme action. Blanching helps retain good color, flavor, texture, and food value. It also cleans and softens the vegetables.

4. Cool quickly; plunge rack in ice water. Chill same amount of time as blanched; drain.

5. Package in moisture-vaporproof containers. Allow for headspace as recommended on page 82.

6. Seal, following manufacturer's directions. Label with contents and date.

7. Freeze in small batches at 0° or less. Frozen vegetables may be stored for 8 to 12 months. Do not refreeze thawed vegetables.

Water and Steam Blanching

Water blanching: Water blanching is the most satisfactory way to prepare practically all vegetables for home freezing. To water blanch, place one pound prepared vegetables in a wire-mesh basket. (A cheesecloth bag or colander will work also. A blancher with a blanching basket and cover makes the job easy.) Immerse the vegetables in basket into one gallon boiling water in large kettle. Cover; boil for time indicated on chart, pages 86 and 87. Start timing at once. Allow 1 minute longer at 5,000 or more feet above sea level.

Steam blanching: Broccoli, pumpkin, sweet potatoes, and winter squash are more satisfactorily steam blanched. Steam blanching takes a little longer than water blanching. To steam blanch, use a kettle with tight lid and a rack three inches off bottom. Add 1 to 2 inches water; bring to rapid boil. Keep heat high. Place vegetables in single layer in basket so steam reaches all parts quickly; lower onto rack. Cover and steam for time indicated on charts, pages 86 and 87. Start counting time immediately. Steam 1 minute longer at 5,000 or more feet above sea level.

Water blanch prepared vegetables in a basket lowered into boiling water, then cooled in ice water for an equal length of time before draining.

Selecting Vegetables for Freezing

Fresh, tender vegetables from the garden are best for freezing. Gather the vegetables early in the morning before they have absorbed much heat, and prepare for freezing immediately or refrigerate till preparation time. Store them only a short time, however, as vegetables should be processed immediately for peak flavor, quality, and food value. Overripe vegetables are tough and flavorless. Some varieties of vegetables freeze better than others, so find out from your County Extension Service which ones are recommended in your locality.

Asparagus	Young; tender stalks; crisp; well-formed, tightly closed tips; about 2 inches light-colored woody base
Beans, green	Young; tender; crisp snap; long, straight pods
Beans, lima	Tender-skinned; crisp; slightly rounded, bright green pods
Beets	Young; not more than 2 to 3 inches in diameter; rounded with smooth, firm flesh
Broccoli	Firm, tender stalks; tight, compact, dark green heads; not woody
Brussels sprouts	Firm, compact, bright green heads; small to medium heads
Carrots	Firm; well-shaped; dark in color; mild flavored
Cauliflower	Firm; tender; snow-white head; heavy, compact head; bright green jacket of leaves
Corn	Young; tender; even rows of plump, milky kernels; fresh, green husk
Greens	Young, tender leaves
Peas, green	Bright green, well-filled pods; plump peas
Potatoes, sweet	Firm texture; smooth; bright; uniform skin color; medium to large
Rutabagas	Roots heavy for size; firm; smooth; small or medium
Squash, summer	Young with small seeds; firm; tender rind; heavy for size; glossy
Squash, winter	Mature; fully colored; firm, hard rind; heavy for size
Turnips	Heavy for size; firm; smooth; fairly round

Freezing Vegetables

Vegetable	Preparation	Blanching	
		Boiling water	Steam (on rack over boiling water)
Asparagus	Wash. Trim; cut to package length or in 2-inch pieces. Sort according to stalk thickness.	Small stalks—2 min. Large stalks—4 min.	

Vegetable	Preparation	Blanching	
		Boiling water	Steam (on rack over boiling water)
Beans, green lima	Wash; remove ends. Cut in 1- or 2-inch pieces, or French cut. Shell. Or leave in pods and shell after blanching.	3 min. Small—2 min. Large—4 min.	
Beets	Wash and sort according to size; leave ½-inch stems. Cook till tender. Peel; cut up.	Small—25 to 30 min. Medium—45 to 50 min.	
Broccoli	Wash; peel stalks; trim; cut into medium pieces 5 to 6 inches long, no thicker than 1½ inches.	3 min.	5 min.
Brussels sprouts	Cut from stem; wash carefully. Remove outer leaves. Sort according to size.	Small—3 min. Large—5 min.	
Carrots	Wash; scrape or peel. Cut into ¼-inch slices or leave whole if small and tender.	Sliced—2 min. Whole—5 min.	
Cauliflower	Wash; cut into 1-inch pieces.	3 min.	
Corn, on cob kernel	Husk; remove silk, wash, and sort. Don't use overmature corn. Blanch ears. Cool; cut off corn.	Small ears—7 min. Medium ears—9 min. Large ears—11 min. 4 min.	
Greens	Wash. Cut and discard thick stems and imperfect leaves.	2 min.	
Mixed vegetables	Prepare. Blanch separately for times given; mix vegetables together after cooling.		
Peas, green	Shell. Discard starchy peas.	1½ min.	
Potatoes, sweet	Cook till almost tender with jackets on. Cool; peel and slice. Dip in solution of ½ cup lemon juice to 1 quart water. Or mash; mix 2 tablespoons lemon juice with each quart.	Cook 30 to 40 min.	Cook 45 to 60 min.
Rutabagas and Turnips	Wash, cut off tops, peel, and cut into ½-inch cubes.	2 min.	
Squash, summer winter	Wash. Cut in ½-inch slices. Cut into pieces; remove seeds. Cook till soft. Remove pulp; mash. Cool quickly.	3 min. Cook 15 min.	Cook about 20 min.

MEAT, POULTRY, AND FISH

Since freezing preserves meat, but doesn't upgrade quality, shopping for top quality is as important as price. Then, use proper wrapping and store at 0° to maintain the goodness.

Meat: High-quality, well-finished animals yield the best frozen meats. For small purchases, watch for specials at the meat counter. For large quantities, consider local locker plants that offer full services including slaughtering, chilling, and quick freezing.

Poultry: Select young, tender birds that have grown quickly and are well-finished.

Fish: Any firm-fleshed, fresh, chilled fish is suitable for freezing.

Steps to proper freezer packaging

Use suitable wrapping paper 1½ times as long as what is needed to go around the particular food. Place food in center of wrapping paper.

Make sure that the coated side of paper is next to the food. Bring wrapping sides together at top. Fold down edges in series of locked folds.

Press wrapping paper against food, then crease both ends to form points. Press wrapping tightly to remove any entrapped pockets of air.

Turn under both pointed ends. Secure ends and the seam with freezer tape. Label packages carefully with contents and date of packaging.

Preparation for Freezing

Meat, poultry, and fish are usually frozen uncooked, but cooked meats, generally leftovers, can be wrapped and frozen too. Cured and smoked meats also freeze satisfactorily for short periods of time. Freeze meat while it is fresh and in the peak of condition. This applies both to cuts purchased at a retail store and to carcass meat slaughtered at home or at a locker plant. Follow directions below:

1. Prepare meat according to chart.

2. Wrap meat in moisture-vaporproof material to prevent freezer burn—drying out of the meat surface. (If you plan to use the meat within 1 to 2 weeks, put prepackaged cuts of meat from the supermarket into the freezer without rewrapping. For longer storage, open the package and rewrap.)

Separate individual portions of chops, patties, or fillets with two pieces of waxed paper, or wrap the portions separately. Cover sharp bones with a double thickness of foil. Mold flexible wrapping materials such as freezer paper, heavy foil, or freezer-weight plastic wrap to the shape of the meat (see diagrams). Remove as much air as possible.

3. Seal with freezer tape and label with the contents, weight or number of servings, and the date the meat was packaged.

4. Freeze quickly at 0° or below in small batches. (Place a single layer of meat in coldest part of freezer.) Keep frozen at constant temperature of 0° or less. Do not refreeze meat once it has thawed.

How to Thaw

Allow several hours for meat, poultry, or fish to thaw before cooking, or add time to the roasting or broiling schedule and cook the meat without thawing.

If time will allow, thaw meats in their freezer wrappings in refrigerator. However, if you're in a hurry, place the tightly wrapped package in cold water (change water often). If you have a microwave oven, follow manufacturer's directions for thawing meat.

Freezing Meat, Poultry, and Fish

Food	Preparation for freezing	How to serve	Storage time
Meat	Have meat cut in desired cuts. Avoid packing more bone than necessary. Wrap the meat tightly in moisture-vaporproof material. Seal, label, and freeze at 0° or below.	Thaw in refrigerator in original wrap.	Beef: 6 to 12 months Lamb and Veal: 6 to 9 months Pork: 3 to 6 months Ground meat: 3 to 4 months Ham: 2 months Bacon: 1 month Cooked meats: 2 to 3 months
Poultry	Chill cleaned, dressed birds. Wrap and freeze giblets separately. Disjoint and cut up bird or leave whole. Wrap bird or pieces in moisture-vaporproof material. Seal, label, and freeze. Never freeze stuffed poultry.	Thaw in refrigerator in original wrap.	Chicken: 12 months Turkey, Duck, Goose: 6 months Giblets: 3 months
Fish	Dress and wash fish. Dip in solution of ⅔ cup salt to 1 gallon water for 30 seconds. Wrap in moisture-vaporproof material. Seal, label, freeze.	Thaw in refrigerator in original wrap or cook frozen, allowing extra time.	Fish: 6 to 9 months
Shellfish	*Oysters, clams, and scallops:* Shuck. Pack in freezer containers; leave ½-inch headspace. Seal, label, freeze. *Crab and lobster:* Cook; chill. Remove meat. Wrap, seal, label, and freeze. *Shrimp:* Freeze uncooked either in shells or shelled. Remove heads. Wrap, seal, label, and freeze.	Thaw in refrigerator in original wrap. Thaw in refrigerator in original wrap. Cook shrimp while still frozen.	Oysters, clams, scallops: 3 months Crabs and Lobster: 1 month Shrimp: 3 months
Eggs	*Whole:* Wash; break into bowl. Stir with fork just to break yolks; mix but don't whip in air. To 1 cup egg, add 1 tablespoon sugar or corn syrup *or* 1 teaspoon salt. Mix; sieve. Pack; skim air bubbles. Leave ½-inch headspace in pints. Seal; label; freeze. *Yolks:* Wash eggs. Separate into bowl. Prepare yolks as for whole eggs, *except* add 2 tablespoons sugar or corn syrup *or* 1 teaspoon salt per cup. *Whites:* Wash eggs. Separate into bowl. Do not stir or add anything to whites. Package the whites exactly as you would whole eggs.	Thaw unopened in refrigerator; use promptly. (2½ table-spoons=1 egg.) Allow for added sugar, corn syrup, or salt. Thaw unopened in refrigerator; use promptly. (1 table-spoon=1 yolk.) Thaw unopened in refrigerator; use promptly. (1½ table-spoons=1 white.)	Whole eggs: 6 to 8 months Egg yolks: 6 to 8 months Egg whites: 6 to 8 months

PREPARED FOODS

Because many prepared foods freeze well, you the homemaker, benefit in two ways. First, you'll save money and last-minute preparation time by planning make-ahead meals or menu items. Second, by freezing these foods, you can make good use of your freezer throughout the year. Refer to the chart on pages 90 to 92 for both preparation instructions and freezer life of individual foods. Use frozen foods during the specified storage time for best flavor, appearance, and texture.

Preparation for Freezing

Except for some types of pies, most mixtures are cooked or partially cooked before freezing. For best results, season food lightly (some flavors intensify in freezing; others decrease), undercook slightly (freezing and reheating soften the structure), and use fat sparingly in sauces (it doesn't blend well when reheated). Add toppers at heating time.

1. Prepare food as shown on pages 90 to 92.

2. Cool the food quickly by placing the pan of cooked food in a sink of ice water.

3. Package the food properly in moisture-vaporproof material. Pack tightly to remove as much air as possible. To save freezer space and to free the dish for reuse, line casserole or pan with heavy foil, leaving long ends. Fill with prepared food, seal foil, and place container in freezer. When food is frozen, remove from container. Reheat foil-wrapped food in same casserole or pan.

4. Seal; label with contents and date.

5. Freeze at 0° or below.

Freezing Prepared Foods

Food	Preparation for freezing	How to serve	Storage time
Breads: Baking powder biscuits	Bake as usual; cool. Seal in freezer container, or wrap in foil and seal.	Thaw in 300° oven about 20 minutes	2 months
Doughnuts	Fry; cool. Wrap and seal.	Reheat in oven.	2 to 4 weeks
Muffins	Bake as usual; cool. Seal in freezer container, or wrap in foil and seal.	Thaw at room temperature 1 hour or in 300° oven about 20 minutes.	2 months
Yeast breads	Bake as usual; cool quickly. Wrap and seal.	Thaw at room temperature for 3 hours.	2 months
Yeast rolls	Use either plain or sweet dough recipe. Bake as usual; cool quickly. Wrap in foil and seal. Freeze at once.	Thaw baked rolls in package at room temperature or in 250° to 300° oven about 15 minutes. Use at once.	2 months
	Or partially bake at 325° about 15 minutes; do not let brown. Cool, wrap, and freeze at once.	Thaw 10 to 15 minutes at room temperature. Unwrap; bake at 450° 5 to 10 minutes.	2 months

Food	Preparation for freezing	How to serve	Storage time
Cakes: General	Bake as usual. Remove from pan; cool thoroughly. If you frost cake, freeze it before wrapping. Wrap; seal. If desired, place in sturdy container. Freeze at once. (Unfrosted cakes freeze better. Frosted and filled cakes may become soggy.)	Thaw wrapped at room temperature 2 to 3 hours (1 hour for layers). If frosted or filled, thaw loosely covered in the refrigerator.	Unfrosted 6 months
Sponge and angel food	Bake as usual; cool thoroughly. If frosted, freeze before wrapping. Then wrap and seal. If desired, place in sturdy container.	Thaw in package 2 to 3 hours at room temperature. If frosted, thaw loosely covered in the refrigerator.	1 month
Cake frostings and fillings	*Recommended:* Frostings with powdered sugar and fat, cooked-candy type with honey or corn syrup, fudge, penuche, fruit, nut. Seal; freeze. *Not recommended:* Soft 7-minute frostings, boiled icings, cream fillings.	Thaw in refrigerator.	2 months
Cookies: Unbaked	Pack dough in freezer containers; seal. *Not recommended:* Meringue-type cookies.	Thaw in package at room temperature till soft. Bake.	6 to 12 months
Baked	Bake as usual; cool. Pack in freezer containers with waxed paper between layers and in air spaces. Seal. Freeze.	Thaw in package at room temperature.	6 to 12 months

Main dishes:
Casseroles:
Poultry,
  fish, or
  meat with
  vegetable
  or pasta
	Cool mixture quickly. Turn into freezer container or casserole. Leave 1-inch headspace. Cover tightly. Seal, label, and freeze.	If frozen in oven-proof container, uncover. Bake at 400° till hot, 1 hour for pints; 1¾ hours for quarts. Or steam in top of double boiler.	2 to 4 months

Creamed Dishes:
Chicken,
  turkey,
  fish, or
  seafood
	Cool quickly. Freeze any except those containing hard-cooked egg white. Don't overcook. Use fat sparingly when making sauce. Leave 1-inch headspace in freezer containers. Cover tightly. Seal; label; freeze.	Heat without thawing in top of double boiler, stirring occasionally. If sauce separates, stir till smooth.	

Meatballs with
  tomato
  sauce
	Cook till done; cool quickly. Ladle into jars or freezer containers, allowing 1-inch headspace. Seal, label, and freeze.	Stir frequently over low heat or occasionally in top of double boiler.	3 months

Prepared Foods (continued)

Food	Preparation for freezing	How to serve	Storage time
Main dishes: (cont.) Meat pies and scalloped dishes	Cook meat till tender. Cook vegetables till almost tender. Cool quickly. Top with pastry, or freeze pastry separately. Wrap tightly. Seal; label; freeze.	Bake frozen pies with pastry topper at 400° for 45 minutes for pints and 1 hour for quarts.	2 to 3 months
Pastry:	Pastry and graham cracker shells freeze satisfactorily. Roll out dough; fit it into pie plates. Bake, if desired. Wrap and seal.	Thaw at 325° for 8 to 10 minutes. Bake unbaked frozen pastry same as fresh.	2 months
Pies: Fruit, general	*Unbaked:* Treat light-colored fruits with ascorbic acid color keeper to prevent darkening. Prepare pie as usual, but don't slit top crust. Use glass or metal pie plate. Cover with inverted pie plate. Wrap and seal. If desired, place in sturdy container. Freeze at once.	Unwrap; cut vent holes in top crust. Without thawing, bake at 450° for 15 to 20 minutes, then at 375° till done. Berry or cherry: Bake at 400°.	2 months
Apple pie, unbaked	Treat with ascorbic acid color keeper or steam apple slices 2 minutes; cool and drain. Prepare as above.	Prepare as above, *except* bake at 425° about 1 hour.	2 months
Peach pie, unbaked	Treat peaches with ascorbic acid color keeper. Prepare as above.	Fix as above, *except* bake at 400° 1 hour.	2 months
Chiffon pie	Chocolate and lemon freeze well.	Thaw in refrigerator.	2 weeks
Sandwiches:	*These freeze well:* Cream cheese, hard-cooked egg yolk, sliced or ground meat, tuna or salmon, peanut butter. Spread bread with butter; fill. Top with second buttered bread slice. Wrap. Seal; label; freeze. *Not recommended:* Lettuce, celery, tomatoes, cucumber, watercress, whites of hard-cooked eggs, jelly, mayonnaise.	Thaw sandwiches in wrapping at room temperature, about 3 hours. Serve immediately.	2 weeks
Stews and soups:	Select vegetables that freeze well. Omit potatoes and onions. Green pepper and garlic intensify in flavor. Omit salt and thickening if stew is to be kept longer than 2 months. Undercook vegetables. Cool quickly; wrap. Seal, label, and freeze.	Heat quickly from frozen state. Do not overcook. Separate with fork as it thaws. Do not stir enough to make mixture mushy.	2 to 4 months

EQUIPMENT FOR FREEZING

The Freezer

Except for the freezer itself, investment in freezing equipment is minimal. The freezer, though, will prove its worth after only a few years of offering convenience as well as saving time, money, and energy. Basically, there are three types of freezers:

Freezer-Refrigerator: Two compartments, one for freezing and one for keeping refrigerated foods, are contained within this appliance. Probably less suited than the other types for the initial freezing of quantities of food, the freezer-refrigerator can store small amounts of frozen food for short periods.

Upright Freezer: Similar in appearance to home refrigerators, upright freezers have one or two outside doors. Uprights are convenient for storing and removing food and require only a small amount of floor space.

Chest or Trunk-Type Freezer: Shaped like a large trunk or chest, the freezer has a top horizontal door opening. Chest-type freezers are suitable for basements or large kitchens.

Place freezers in a cool, dry, well-ventilated location. The temperature inside the freezer should be 0° or below at all times. Check periodically by keeping a freezer thermometer in freezer. Follow the manufacturer's directions for care and defrosting.

Containers and Wraps

All containers and wrapping materials for freezing must be moisture-vaporproof to retain highest quality in frozen foods. Other important characteristics include durability; resistance to oil, grease, and water; and ease of labeling. Choose the flexible wrapping or rigid container appropriate for the particular food that you wish to package.

Flexible wrappings are those that mold to the food's shape. They include sheet wraps such as heavy foil, cellophane, plastic, and laminated paper. Heavy plastic or foil bags can be used too. Dry-packed vegetables, fruits, and meats can be satisfactorily wrapped and frozen in flexible materials.

In case of power failure

Do not open freezer or remove food if electricity is off. Food will stay frozen for approximately 2 days.

If power is out longer, put dry ice in freezer (allow 2½ pounds per cubic foot) or move food to a commercial locker.

All packages should have an airtight seal. Follow directions on page 88 for proper wrapping method. Use special freezer tape to ensure air tightness of sheet-wrapped packages. Tie bags shut with freezer wire or a rubber band. Label package with contents and date.

Rigid containers, although suitable for all packs, are especially good for liquids. The containers are made of metal, plastic, heavily waxed cardboard, or glass. Most are reusable. Make sure lids fit securely for an airtight seal. Label with contents and date. Use a wax crayon or write on freezer tape.

Choose rigid containers that are easy to handle and pack in the freezer. Containers that have straight sides and stackable tops and bottoms save freezer space. Pack food in portions for one meal.

Preparation Equipment

Having a few special utensils in addition to regular kitchen equipment will make freezing easier and more successful.

A measuring scale takes away the measuring guesswork. Funnels of different sizes aid in adding syrup and filling containers. And a blancher with a special blanching basket and cover makes freezing vegetables easier and quicker. You might also want a meat saw.

Additional large pans may be needed for preparing big quantities of food. Other regular equipment includes timer, paring knives, cutting board, wooden and metal spoons, and measuring spoons and cups.

INDEX

Foods are canned unless freezing is specified. *Indicates canned foods are used in a recipe.